SINGING AWAY
THE HUNGER

Mpho 'M'atsepo Nthunya, 1994.   Photograph: K. Kendall

SINGING AWAY THE HUNGER

THE AUTOBIOGRAPHY OF AN AFRICAN WOMAN

MPHO 'M'ATSEPO NTHUNYA

EDITED BY K. LIMAKATSO KENDALL
WITH A FOREWORD BY ELLEN KUZWAYO

INDIANA UNIVERSITY PRESS
BLOOMINGTON AND INDIANAPOLIS

First Indiana University Press edition 1997

Singing Away the Hunger was originally published in South Africa by the University of Natal Press. The North American edition is being made available by special arrangement.

© 1996 by Mpho 'M'atsepo Nthunya

Three of these stories ("South African Police," "When a Woman Loves a Woman," and "The Snow Was So Cold It Was Blue") were first published in *Basali! Stories by and about Women in Lesotho* (University of Natal Press, 1995). "The Child Is Burning" was first published in *Na Le Oena* (NUL Publishing House, 1995).

The paper used in this publication meets the minimum requirements of American National Standard for Information Sciences—Permanence of Paper for Printed Library Materials, ANSI Z39.48-1984.

Manufactured in the United States of America

Library of Congress Cataloging-in-Publication Data

Nthunya, Mpho 'M'atsepo, date
    Singing away the hunger : the autobiography of an African woman/ Mpho 'M'atsepo Nthunya ; edited by K. Limakatso Kendall ; with a foreword by Ellen Kuzwayo.
        p.   cm.
    ISBN 0-253-33352-0 (alk. paper). — ISBN 0-253-21162-X (pbk. : alk. paper)
    1. Nthunya, Mpho 'M'atsepo, date. 2. Lesotho—Biography. 3. Women, Sotho—Lesotho—Biography. 4. Sotho (African people) —Lesotho—Social life and customs.   I. Kendall, K. Limakatso. II. Title.
CT1938.N77A3   1997
968.85'02'092—dc21
[B]   97-18778

1 2 3 4 5 02 01 00 99 98 97

NTHUNYA, MPHO

ORDER NO:
ORDER DATE: 29JUN1999

SINGING AWAY THE HUNGER : THE AUTOBIOGRAPHY OF F
AN AFRICAN WOMAN / MPHO 'M'ATSEPO NTHUNYA ;
EDITED

INDIANA UNIVERSITY PRE 1997   1 VOLS   O
87-019780   35.00 CLOTH   R
0-253-33352-0 07-18778   D

QTY ORDERED: 001   E
QTY SHIPPED: 001   R

BLACKWELL BOOK SERVICES   660305/0002

Contents

Illustrations

Some of the photographs in this book are from Mpho Nthunya's own album. The pictures on Plates One to Six are included because of their striking likeness to the people and places in her memory. The University of Natal Press acknowledges with gratitude the institutions and individuals who made photographs available, particularly those who did not charge a fee for reproduction.

Acknowledgements

Mpho Nthunya and Kendall are grateful to the Fulbright Foundation of the USA, for the material support that brought us together for this work; we also acknowledge the spiritual support of Mpho's mother, Valeria 'M'amahlaku Sekobi Lillane; and Kendall's grandmother, Olive Kendall Weedon Dermid. Barbara Jordan, of the LBJ School of Public Affairs in Texas, loved the manuscript and believed in it, and it grieves us that she died before it became a book; we miss her. In addition we want publicly to thank all the people who read and commented on the stories between 1992 and 1995 and insisted we must find a publisher. Notable among those are Anne Eberle, who helped us in many ways, and Jane Garrett, Tai Hazard, Joan Lennox, Jeannine Haas, Patricia Sipe, Julia Chere-Masopha, Mafina Mphuthing, Muso and Mathankiso Nthunya, A.E. McQueen, Seth Kendall, Leslie Canaan (who dreams of directing a movie made from the book), and Chris Dunton. We thank Trish Comrie for the care and perseverance with which she converted Kendall's computer disks into galley proofs and final pages and eliminated the Americanisms. Our fondest thanks go to Margery Moberly, Head of the University of Natal Press, who wanted to publish the stories from the moment she heard about them in January 1995. Her soaring enthusiasm for this work, added to her lifelong interest in African women's stories, and twenty years of expertise in publishing, made the book a reality.

Foreword

By Ellen Kuzwayo (*Member of Parliament*)

This book by Mpho Nthunya brings back memories of my early childhood. It takes me back nearly seventy years, to my childhood on my maternal grandfather's farm in Thaba Patchoa, in the Orange Free State, approximately a hundred and fifty miles from Lesotho. I spoke Setswana at school; however, as most of my playmates on that farm were children of farm workers who came from Lesotho, Sesotho became my second language and the Basotho culture, my second culture. One has a tendency, in looking back, to feel nostalgia for days gone by, but these stories of Basotho people's lives are too shocking, one might even say brutal, to feed that longing for times past. I have been reading Mpho Nthunya's stories in the midst of a bitter winter with unusually heavy snowfalls in South Africa; and I have been feeling great sympathy for people in the Maluti Mountains of Lesotho, where the winters are more severe than anything we ever experience in South Africa.

Many South Africans are aware that Basotho migrant workers have laboured in our mines for many years, but the Basotho people have contributed to our country's riches in other ways. They also worked on farms owned by wealthy people of Becwana origin. To this day, much of the cash income in Lesotho is money paid to migrant workers – women and men alike, employed in domestic work, on farms, in factories and of course in the mines. Such workers, even today, earn very low wages. The migrant system as it has functioned in South Africa has been responsible for the breakdown of countless Basotho families, for the economic exploitation and abuse of generations of Basotho people, and for the continuing poverty which devastates Lesotho. It would be reasonable, given this history, for a Mosotho to tell the history of her life, her country, with justifiable rage.

Therefore I have been both amazed and impressed by Mpho Nthunya's writing, which is spare and factual; her stories are not anywhere touched by emotions of sorrow, self-pity, anger, or revenge. Her calmness of mind and thought is inspiring. For example, when thieves rob her of her sheep and goats, she tells that fact without judgment; the bitterness, anger or frustration is thus in the reader, not in the author. That is her artistry: she *shows* us what her life has been and allows the reactions to take place in us, as we read.

Similarly her response to her husband's illness and death reveal Mpho's deep-seated courage, love and devotion to a man who laid down his life for his family. On first reading, Mpho may strike the reader of this story as over-trusting and submissive. Why, we might ask, didn't she fight back? Why didn't she stand her ground? When her husband, Alexis, appointed a relative of his to receive and supervise the pension or disability money he earned from his employment, that relative stole the money from the very mouths of Alexis's children. This, to me, indicates lack of trust in women, particularly where family wealth is concerned. Why didn't Alexis have the money sent directly to his wife? Why didn't Mpho fight that relative for her money and her children's money? The readers of her stories are left with these questions, and with the frustration that comes with them. Her stories suggest the need for action, and they leave the reader wanting to make changes. Perhaps this is what is most 'radical' about the book. It is a call to action.

Some women have had to over-surrender themselves to gain protection; they pay a great deal in terms of autonomy in order to satisfy various African traditions or expectations of women. To me, Mpho Nthunya's book mirrors women's vulnerability where major issues of their lives are concerned. True as it is that many African women have overcome untold obstacles and challenges to make ends meet, to achieve some small semblance of security; that state of affairs must not be allowed to continue. The stories in *Singing Away the Hunger* must be accepted as a call for change. Women in all communities need to be helped to develop individual self-respect, dignity and above all self-reliance. Women must be helped to stand up for their rights without undermining their menfolk. This book calls us to that way forward.

As I read of the decision Mpho and her husband made, to leave Benoni Location near Johannesburg, where they were making a living, and to return to the harsh poverty of life in the Maluti Mountains, I kept asking myself why they would do that. Was it their deep love of their country? Mpho describes ably and clearly how harsh life was in the Maluti without ever saying that life was harsh. Her stories create vivid pictures: old men weaving baskets to sell in the valleys; women making clothes by hand or on hand-operated machines; families having major disturbances over the disappearance of a few cups of sugar; women growing dark and thin on hard labour and little food; children dying from lack of medical care and from malnutrition. Why, then, would any couple in its right mind choose to pack up their children and go there? The vicious laws of apartheid, the crowding and crime and noise of the townships had to be balanced, by this young couple, against the possibility of starvation in the mountains. The wide quiet Mpho describes, the space, the sky and the mountains seem to have been enough of an answer for her. But her stories force us to ask why any people should have to choose between such unacceptable options.

What also emerges in the stories is Mpho's independence, her resilience, her determination to make a life of her own choosing, confined as that choosing was to the narrow range of choices available to her. We also get glimpses of Mpho's rebelliousness. Not for her, the placid acceptance of her own mother. 'I was sometimes fed up with her,' Mpho admits; and then she tells us she told her mother, 'If I was you, in those hard years when my father was not sending us any money, I was not going to wear a sack and wait for him and pray. I was going to leave, and see if I can find work in Gauteng.' Even more powerfully, 'If I was married to a man who hit me, I was not going to stay and let him do it, and say prayers for him to stop. I was going to leave him and keep on praying for help while I was leaving.' Mpho tells us her mother bore up humbly under her sufferings, saying, 'I will carry this load.' But Mpho says, 'I thought it was a good thing it was her, and not me, because I was not going to carry it at all. I was going to find a way out.' Mpho does not in any way insult or demean her mother's behaviour; she just makes it clear that she wouldn't have put up with those sufferings. She has the ability to review a situation and to separate good from bad, using what is best for her benefit.

It took outstanding character and personality for Mpho Nthunya to forge a life for herself and her family and then to bring up six children after her husband's death. It takes outstanding character and courage for a woman to dare to tell the truth about her life. This book shows that. Mpho's humility is moving. Time and again she expresses doubt about her book, doubt as to its appeal to readers, Basotho or non-Basotho. It is a simple book, but a great book, and part of its greatness is the questions it forces us to ask: about our societies, our values, the sets of choices we now refer to as 'lifestyles'; and about the lives of women and men in colonised African communities. In its unembroidered telling of the facts of life for one poor but resourceful African woman, it reaches out to people of all races, classes and backgrounds; to the educated and to people like Mpho herself: the African women of the earth, so often referred to as women at the grass roots of society. One hopes she will live to see the success of this book and perhaps to write another, for she has much to tell us all.

National Assembly
Cape Town

CHAPTER 1

Before the Beginning

Making this book is a strange thing to me: in Sesotho we say *mohlolo* – a miracle, or a wonder. Most of the people in my life – my family, my friends, my neighbours – most of them cannot read. Almost none of them can read English. You go into any house in my neighbourhood, and you will not find a book, unless it is one of the children's school-books, wrapped in brown paper the way the nuns tell them to do it. Books are not part of our lives.

Even me: I can read English because I learned it in a school in Benoni Location, in the Union of South Africa, when I was a girl. I like books very much; when I see a book I always want to know what's in it, especially if it has pictures. But I have no time to read anything. If I am at home, the children are coming in and going out and needing things all the time. At the end of the day I am so tired all I can do is sleep. If I am at work, my arms are in soapy water or I'm ironing or cleaning the floors. When can I read? I see that some of the young Basotho like to read books; I see a young person sometimes with a book that's not even for school. I am glad for that. But the people of Mafikeng, where I live, will never read my book. It will not mean anything to them.

I am telling my stories in English for many months now, and it is a time for me to see my whole life. I see that things are always changing. I was born in 1930, so I remember many things which were happening in the old days in Lesotho and which happen no more. I lived in Benoni Location for more than ten years, and I saw the Boer policemen taking the black people and beating them like dogs. They even took me once, and kept me in one of their jails for a while.

I was married with a good Mosotho man, and we left Benoni and lived in the Maluti Mountains where we had many children, raised sheep, grew maize, and listened to the quiet. At the beginning we were hungry and our children were hungry; but after many years of working hard we were no longer poor. We had many animals and fields. Then my husband died, and I had to come back to my mother's home, in the Roma Valley, to find work. I lost or sold the animals and left the fields and my houses in the mountains. Now I live in Mafikeng, the village at the gates of the National University of Lesotho. I have worked at the University cleaning houses since 1968. It is at the University that I meet Limakatso, I call her *motsoalle oa ka*, my very good friend. I tell her my stories and she writes them down in a computer to make them a book. *Mohlolo!*

Talking to Limakatso, I remember many things which I forgot for a long time. This is a good thing for me. I'm looking back, and it's like looking at an album of photos from my whole life. If other people can look at it too, that's fine. But it's my album, and it pleases me to look at it. I'm telling stories for children and grown people in other places, because I want people who know how to read and have time to read, to know something about the Basotho – how we used to live and how we live now, how poor we are, and how we are living together in this place called Lesotho. I'm also telling stories for Basotho like my grandchildren, who read books but don't know the old ways of their own people. If they can read these stories, maybe it will teach them where they come from. And maybe it can help them to learn English, so they can find work.

I tell these stories in English to my *motsoalle* so she can write them in the computer. I can tell these stories better in Sesotho. When I tell stories in Sesotho, the words roll like a music I am singing with my heart. When I speak *Sekhooa*, the white people's language, I start and stop. I stare at my *motsoalle*, at the ceiling, looking, looking. I say, 'What can I say? What is the word for this?'

I am like a car trying to start on a cold morning, coughing and stopping. Limakatso says people who read *Sekhooa* never get to hear the stories from women like me, and I think it must be true.

When would we write them? I have only a Standard Five education, went to Standard Six for a little while but didn't finish it. I don't know the people who publish books, don't know where to send a book if I could write it. Limakatso says people are hungry for these stories. They want to know. So I say, '*Ho lokile. Fine.* It's OK with me. We can write them.' Maybe I make a little bit of money to buy maize meal for the children.

I try to imagine what I can do with a book written by me. I think of my mother. I imagine that I can give this book of English words to her, and because of the wisdom of Heaven she can read it. I say to her, 'Take this book and see your story: when you were married, and what happened to your daughter, who always loves you. Here are the stories of your daughter's children, and their children. None of this would be, without you. And now others can know your story.' So I say this book is my album for my mother, Valeria 'M'amahlaku Sekobi Lillane, who passed away. Others can look at it if they like.

CHAPTER 2

Death by Novena

My mother's family was not Christian. Her mother was always drinking *joala*, and her father was very cruel. When the parents came together, there was always a quarrel, so my mother was not happy in her heart to stay at home. When the Roman Catholic mission opened a school for children, my mother asked to go. It was a free school, then; there were no school fees, so maybe her parents thought it was good to give her something to do in the daytime so she was out of their way, and they let her go.

When my mother began school at Roma, two French Catholic fathers were there: *Ntate* Bernard and *Ntate* Gerard. *Ntate* Bernard used to come to the classrooms and talk about prayers and teach the students how to pray. My mother liked this.

One day she went to Father Bernard and told him about her mother and father and the fighting in their house. So Father Bernard gave her a rosary and taught her how to pray. And Father Bernard told her that you can't do anything without praying. He said, 'You say your father is cruel and your family is not good. You can help your parents by praying.' He gave her a paper with prayers to be said for Novena, and he taught her how to pray for nine days. She did what he told her, made the prayers for nine days, and by the end of the nine days that Novena made my mother to be a Christian. Her mother didn't care. She was only drinking *joala*. She didn't mind what Valeria did, and her father didn't pay any attention.

So my mother told me she took this paper, and she used to pray with this paper and a rosary, and she said her prayers changed the way she felt about her family, which made life better for her. She said the most important thing she learned is that you must love everybody like yourself. So my mother was like that. She liked everybody. If someone insulted her, or took something that belonged to her, she didn't care. She said to turn the other cheek. Even if somebody beat me, she didn't go and quarrel with that person, and ask them, 'Why do you beat my child?' No. She would just say to me, 'OK, my child, it's nothing. You won't die.' I was sometimes fed up with her when she said this, because I would see other children, when somebody beats them, their mothers go and quarrel, and argue. Me, I just have to cry and wipe my own tears, because I know there is no use to go to my mother. So I didn't like this Christianity of hers, when I was a child. But people liked my mother, because she liked them and because she was kind.

When I grew up, I saw that my mother's religion is good for me. I came to understand that prayer is a way to see God. I have many troubles, but when I pray and I see God, the troubles pass away from my heart. When my sons die, I know it's time for them to go and see God, and even myself, I know that I am going to die. I am not afraid to die because I see that everybody is going to die. So if you die, it's your time to die. If it's not your time, God won't allow you to die. This is good for me because it makes me not to be living my life afraid. I pray the rosary and say Novena sometimes, but I can't do it for nine days, like my mother. She taught me a short Novena, because she saw I am not like her – I can keep going every day for three days, or maybe six, but not nine. I'm not like her.

She was very beautiful, very dark-skinned, with a long face and a nice figure. She was short, like me, and she wore size four shoes. She had long fingers and strong hands. Many people said how beautiful she was.

I told her, 'If I was you, in those hard years when my father was not sending us any money, I was not going to wear a sack and wait for him and pray. I was going to leave, and see if I can find work in Gauteng. I wouldn't stay here.' I always said so, when she would talk about those years. And I said if I was married to a man who hit me, I was not going to stay and let him do it, and say prayers for him to stop. I was going to leave him and keep on praying for help while I was leaving.

So she would tell me I have no Christian life in my heart. She said to me, 'You don't trust God. You put your trust in yourself, so you can't be surprised if God doesn't answer your prayers.' My mother told me many stories about how prayer helped her when there was trouble in her family, like the time she was almost forced to marry a man she didn't even know. This is the story she told me.

When I was a girl, my father was a very cruel man, but I knew how to stand up to him. One day there came a man with a horse. He came from a little village in the mountains, Ha Teko, near Molimo Nthuse. He greeted my father and they said the usual things. My father took a chair and gave it to this man outside the house and they sat down to talk. I stood close enough that I could hear them, and the visitor said, 'We want your daughter. My son wants to marry your daughter.'

Ntate listened and didn't say anything to me. He just said, 'Yes, OK. What I want is the *lobola*, that's all. Many cattle.'

I was very excited when I heard this talking. And after talking, the man went back to his horse and rode away.

Ntate called my mother and told her, 'Did you see this man? He wants this daughter of yours. And I said Yes, he can come and bring *lobola*.'

My mother said, 'But she doesn't know the man. How can you take a *lobola*? Here are two children who don't know each other. How can you make a marriage between them?'

Ntate said, 'You are talking rubbish. This daughter can't say anything. I don't care what she wants. I want her to go to Ha Teko, and that's all.'

Ntate came to me and said, 'This man who was here wants you. And I say everything is all right, and I don't want any answer from you. You are going there.'

I didn't answer. I was just quiet. I said in my heart, 'What can I do, because I don't know this man?' But my father says Yes, I must go. I'll try to pray again.

After one week I saw my mother making many *joala* in the house; people came and helped her to make *joala* for the coming of *lobola*. So I went to school that day; I didn't know what was happening, I just saw the *joala* in the house. When I was on the way home from school I met many people walking, going home from Mafikeng to Mafefoane, and I asked one of them what was happening. That lady told me, 'Oh child, your house is so nice, so pretty and nice the way your mother has fixed it up, and those cows that came for your *lobola* are wonderful, fat cows.'

So I realized the *lobola* came that day. This was the first I knew about it.

I was angry. I didn't even answer that lady, because she didn't know what was happening. She didn't know my parents didn't tell me about the feast, or the *lobola*. When I arrived at home I found many people there, drinking *joala*. Even some people from Ha Teko were there. I didn't know if one of them was the man they wanted me to marry or not. I just passed them and went to my grandmother's house. *Nkhono* was not there, but I went into the house and stayed there because I just wanted to hide.

So when the feast was finished and most of the people went home, I came home to find my father drunk. He told me, very harsh, 'Did you see the cattle which marry you? I like them.'

At first I didn't answer, but after a time I said softly, 'I don't like that man, because I don't know him.'

Ntate said, 'You will see him. He will come.'

A month later, my man and a few other boys from Ha Teko were supposed to come. On that day I dressed in my nicest dress, and I sat in the house with three other girls, waiting for the gentlemen to come.

They came on horseback. They entered the house and took seats facing us. We were all very quiet and shy. One of these three men said to me, 'Here is your husband.'

I look at him and I say, 'I don't like him.'

Then the other girls talk with him, trying to be polite, and they say, 'Valeria, don't say you don't like him. You don't know him yet.'

But I say again, 'I don't like him.'

The girls say, 'Your father is going to beat you.'

'It's better to die,' I tell them. 'I don't like him. Maybe my father cares about those cattle more than he cares about me anyway. If my father can keep the cattle, he won't care whether I'm dead or married. I can die before I will live with this man.'

So one of those gentlemen goes out and tells *Ntate*, 'Oh, we are going, *Ntate*, because the lady says she doesn't like this man.'

Then my father comes in the house and shouts at me, '*Hei!* What are you saying, girl? Did you say you don't like this man?'

I say Yes.

He says, 'You are going to Ha Teko. You are going there. These gentlemen can leave today, but when it is time for you to marry this man, you are going.'

He told the men not to mind about me, gave them food. They ate, and they left. They didn't know what to say or what to think.

Then I prayed, telling God that I don't like this man. I said 'It's better to me, God, if I can die.' But I told God I don't want to be sick a long time. Just let me have a pain in the chest, and I will say, softly, 'It's my chest, this pain,' and after that, I die. I heard about people who died this way, and I prayed for that, and I made a Novena for nine days, going to Mass every day in the morning. On the ninth day there came a boy on a horse from Ha Teko. He said to my father,

'*Ntate*, I have come to tell you that the man who was supposed to marry your daughter passed away yesterday.'

'Oh,' my father said, 'What happened?'

'We don't know. He started vomiting blood, and he said he had a pain in the chest. Then he suddenly passed away.'

I was listening, and I could not believe what I heard. I said in my heart, 'Oh God, why didn't you take me, and not that man? I didn't mean for any bad thing to come to him.'

My father came and told me, 'Your husband passed away yesterday, but you are still going to Ha Teko, because I am not going to give these cows back. I like them. If there is another boy in that family, he will take you.'

I just said OK. I didn't answer anything. I said I will just pray to God. I won't talk with this cruel father of mine; I will just go to Mass every day and ask God to help me.

There came another man on a horse and he said, 'What shall we do now, old man? Your daughter said she didn't want our son, and our son has passed away. Maybe we must take back our cows.'

Ntate says, 'Is there another boy in your house?'

'Yes, but he is still young, only seventeen years old.'

'Fine,' my father says. 'She is going to marry him.'

I was twenty-two years old at that time. I listened, and I felt angry, but I didn't speak one word.

So the man from Ha Teko says, 'The boy will come and see the lady soon. We shall see what is going to happen.'

Then came the boy one day with another man, and they sat in the house, waiting. My father called me. I came. I sat down on the mat, not saying anything. The older man from Ha Teko said, 'This is your husband, now, because your first man passed away before you could be married.'

I just looked at them. I saw the one they called my husband was a child still, and I told them I didn't like him.

My father was standing there, and he said, 'You must be mad.' He couldn't think of anything else to say, so he said again, 'You must be mad!'

I just sat quietly, looking down at my hands in my lap. And my father started to shout, 'I say to you, you are still going to Ha Teko. Boy,' he says, asking this child they call my husband, 'do you love this girl?'

The boy says, 'Because she says she doesn't love me, I don't love her too.' And he walked out of the house and looked at the sky.

My father began to sound like a madman. He shouted again at me, 'You are going to Ha Teko!' And he followed the boy outside and told him, 'I won't talk with you because you are too young. I waste my breath trying to talk with children, both of you. Tell your father to come and talk with me, and we will settle this mess. I don't want these cattle to go away, do you hear? I like them.'

I started to pray again, pray again, 'Oh God I don't want to be married with this child.' And I saw my father was worried, always worried.

One day he yelled at my mother and said, 'You must teach this child of yours that when I speak, she must not answer me back. She has nothing to say about any of this, and she is not to answer me back, totally. She is going to Ha Teko and that's all.'

I didn't answer him, but I trusted that God would help me. I was praying every day, all day. My father began to be so worried about those cows, he started talking alone. He would walk up and down outside the house, saying the same things all the time:

'She is going to Ha Teko. These cows are not going back.' One afternoon he took his chair, sat down in the shade of the tree, and while he was talking to himself he just stopped breathing. Passed away. He was dead. And everything was finished.

That was the story my mother told me. I don't know what happened with the *lobola*, but Valeria never went to Ha Teko. I don't think she ever even saw the place in her life. But she never doubted the power of prayer after that.

My mother met *Ntate* Johannes, the man who was going to be my father, in the church when they were in school together. He came from Mokhokhong to school in Roma. He was twenty-four and my mother was twenty-three when they came to love each other, and they asked to be married in the church. But even that was strange.

The day before their wedding, at the end of the Mass, Father Bernard said, 'All people sit down. I want to give you a talk. Since I became a priest, I have never made a marriage like this one which we are going to recognise tomorrow. These two good people love each other, and they are both Christians. But last night when I was sleeping I was shown in a dream that this marriage is going to be hard, very hard. However, I am sure of this girl, Valeria. I know that she is going to carry this heavy load which will be given to her. I'm ashamed to tell you what was shown to me this night. I can't even tell you how much trouble these people are going to have, because all of you can cry in this church if I tell you. But know that whatever happens, this young woman can carry what is given to her.'

So the Mass ended and my mother was wondering what the Father meant. She thought, 'Am I going to die, or what? What can be that bad?'

But later she said when she was at Mokhokhong, wearing a sack and grinding corn all day, and when I was almost burned to death and we were eating grass, she remembered all that the father said. She told me, 'Father Bernard said this is the sacrifice which I am supposed to make, and I will make it. These are my sufferings, which Father Bernard was shown on the night before my wedding, and I will carry this load.' I thought it was a good thing it was her, and not me, because I was not going to carry it at all. I was going to find a way out. But that is the kind of woman my mother was.

Once after my mother died, she came to me in a dream, with a group of ladies who were dead, all of them in the St. Anne Society. She came to me, and she wanted to catch me with her hand, and she tried to kiss me. I said, 'No, *'M'e*, I don't want to die. I know when you kiss me you want to take me. My children are still small. It isn't time for me yet.'

She laughed and said, 'Yes, I wanted to take you, but I thought you didn't know I was coming to take you.'

Many times while I was growing up, she said, 'If God hears me, I want when I die, you shall die and go with me.'

That's why after she died she came back after only one month to take me. She loves me. She is still with me, even now.

CHAPTER 3

The Child is Burning!

When I was my grandson Tumisang's age, about four, it was my time to see that my mother and I were not like others. We lived alone in a very small rondavel, near to my father's mother. She had a nice rondavel and a square house we call a *huisie*, and my brother, who was older than me, lived with her, her daughter, and her daughter's two children. But my mother and I lived alone and we had nothing to eat, nothing to wear. My mother was wearing a rough hessian sack that feels like straw. She wore it in place of a dress or blanket. She had no scarf or *doek* for her head, no shoes. I was the same way.

One day the herdboys saw my mother and me gathering wild *moroho* and singing a church song, *Kabelo ea ka entle*. It was a hymn of the Roman Catholic church, and my mother loved to sing this. But when the herdboys saw us they ran home and told their parents there was a mad woman in the hills, with a baby on her back and a little girl at her side, wearing a sack on her shoulders. The parents told these boys, 'No. She's not mad. She's just poor. You know this woman. She is Valeria Lillane.'

'Then why does she put a sack on her back?'

'Because she have no blanket, my children.'

So the herdboys listened, but they were still afraid to go near us. And when I saw this, I came to know that we were different from the families of those herdboys, and from others in the village.

In the morning my mother wakes up, puts the sack over her shoulders, and goes to the Chief's house to grind maize with a *leloala*, a grinding stone. After she grinds all day to make meal for the Chief, the Chief's wife gives her a handful of maize kernels for her pay. Just a handful. Then she goes to the field to gather the wild *moroho*. She takes the whole day, grinding maize and gathering greens. I'll be sitting at home, under a tree by our little rondavel, playing alone, sleeping, waking up alone. I was wearing a sheepskin over my shoulders and a *thethana*, a little skirt of string. No shoes. My grandmother Lillane is there, but she loved only my brother, Sephefu, the first one, not me. She says I am not my father's child. If I cry, she beats me. So I was not using to cry.

My mother says, 'Don't go to your grandmother. She doesn't love you. She loves her daughter's children, and your brother, but she doesn't like you. So don't go to her.' *Nkhono* did not like my mother, either. I don't know why. Many women don't like their daughter-in-law.

Sephefu felt shame when he saw me sitting near the door, hungry. He was working for my grandmother as a shepherd, and when he brought in the sheep and goats in the afternoon, my grandmother gave him *papa*, maybe with milk. Many times he would try to sneak outside to eat it, so he can give me a little taste, but if she catches him she will say, very harsh, 'Why do you sit outside to eat? What do you want outside? You want to feed your sister, I know. Go back inside the house!' And she shouts at him. If he feeds me she will hit him like a dog.

One day my grandmother was away, and my brother took *papa* and hid it under his blanket to go and give to me. But one of these children saw him. When my grandmother arrived the children said, '*Nkhono*, Sephefu gave Mpho *papa*. He hid it under his blanket and gave it to her and ran away. We saw him.'

So our uncle, the son of our grandmother who came after my father, caught my brother and beat him. In the evening when my mother came home late after dark, I told her my brother was beaten.

My mother said, 'He must leave you alone. You can't die. I ask my God to feed you the whole day. You can't die, I say. Just wait.' And it was true. There was no food, but I did not feel too hungry. When she came home, my mother would ask me, 'Are you hungry, Mpho?'

And I would say, 'Not so bad.'

Then she says, 'Yes, God feeds you. I still feel bad, because you are a child, but what can I do? Nothing to do.'

That day my mother calls my brother and says to him, 'You must not give Mpho anything. God will feed her. She will not die.' My brother is crying, but my mother says, 'Don't cry. They will beat you if you cry.'

He says, 'I cry because this is my sister, and I know she is hungry. I'm working for this *Nkhono*, taking care of her goats and sheep, and she gives me three goats if I work six months; a cow if I work a year. They say, "These are your goats, your cow." But the goats and the cow that are mine, they stay with the others that belong to *Nkhono*. When they slaughter the ones that are mine, I can eat with them, and they eat, but they give nothing to me for you and Mpho. I am ashamed when they slaughter my goat, and I cannot give you even a small piece of it to eat.'

Our mother always said, 'Don't mind, my child, don't mind.'

One time my grandmother was in her house, making a fire with dung. I could see from outside, the fire was very dark and there was much smoke in the house. *Nkhono* calls me to come sit by the fire, and I am surprised. She doesn't call me to her house, even when I am very cold. But I think maybe this time her heart is a little softer to me, and I go. I can't see *Nkhono* in the house, there is so much smoke, and I sit nicely by the fire, trying to be warm, looking into the darkness to see *Nkhono*, seeing only smoke.

Suddenly a piece of the fire leaps out and lands on my little dress from the Roma mission. The fire begins at the bottom of my dress, and I jump up, try to shake it off. The flames and the smoke start to blow up to my face. I run out of the house – run, run, and am calling to my mother. I am running, falling, and screaming. The fire is eating me, I am blind from the fire, and the fire comes more and more.

A neighbour sees me running and calls, ''*M'e* 'M'ampho, the child is burning! The child is burning!'

My grandmother is close by, but she does nothing. My mother is collecting wood in the forest. She leaves the wood and comes running to me, crying, running and falling down, running and stumbling over the stones. And I am running and falling and burning and screaming. My mother catches me and wraps me in the sack she has on her shoulders like a blanket, and she puts out the fire in my clothes.

I was so burned, the dress was stuck to my skin from my ribs to my leg. We had no money to go to a doctor. We just put Basotho medicine on me. My mother took a thick leaf of an aloe and broke it, and squeezed it out on to my burns. She also took another plant, we call it *tikamotse*, and she burned the leaves and took the ash from the leaves and dusted it like a powder over my wounds. And slowly, slowly, over many months, I began to heal. I used to lie down in our little rondavel on my goatskin. I would lie there alone all day with no food while my mother worked for the Chief's wife, grinding maize into meal.

One day came another lady, said to my mother, ''*M'e* 'M'ampho, you must take this child to the hospital in Roma.' We were living in Mokhokong, and my mother was afraid to come to Roma because she had no blanket, only a sack. So the lady borrow her a blanket and put the sack outside her house. It was a thin blanket, but it was the best that lady had. She was poor too. So she let my mother use it, and she gave my mother fifteen cents. My mother went to Roma and bought a medicine which was yellow like the yolk of an egg.

When my mother came home she washed me, washed me all over and put this medicine on my stomach. And in time I came to be better. But later, when I was pregnant the first time, my stomach was very sore where the burn scar was. They say it's because of scar tissue from this wound. I wonder how many Basotho children die in such a way, because my own children were locked into a small house with a dung fire by an uncle who was cruel. But that is another story for later. I still have the scar from that burn. It has shrunk now, to about the size of two hands open wide.

When I got enough better from the burn that I could go out into the fields with my mother again, I would help her cut grass. We were eating grass at that time. We cut it, pounded it with a stick to remove the tiny seeds, and my mother ground these seeds to a kind of meal to make *papa*. It was not tasting nice, but it was all we had. It tasted like *mobu*, dirt, but it was enough to keep us alive.

Then came a sickness that made many people blind. Not blind forever, but blind for a time. My mother got this blindness, too. And one day there were many locusts. The ground was covered with them, flying, and hopping, bumping into each other, like the whole ground was alive. The people were happy to see this, because they could catch the locusts and eat them. My mother could not see them to catch them because of the blindness, and she said, 'Mpho, how can I catch them? I can't see.'

I say, 'Let's go. I am better now. I will help you.'

And we go. We catch them, put them in the sack, and we go home and we eat like other people. And this time I am happy because we are not so different. We are eating like the others.

CHAPTER 4

To Sing the Hunger Away

Many times I heard my mother tell the story of how we arrived in Benoni Location, in Gauteng, because of a dream that came three times. I loved to hear the story, because I was remembering it too, just the way my mother told it, and I have told it to my children and my grandchildren the same way.

We lived at Mokhokhong in a little rondavel near my father's mother until 1938, when we took the first step toward Benoni, which was Roma. We didn't know it was a first step to anywhere. My mother's uncle, who lived in the Roma Valley, sent for my mother to come to him. She was afraid to come to Roma because of not having clothes. When she would come to church in a sack, the people would run away. They didn't want to sit near her. My uncle heard she was wearing this sack and eating grass, and he felt pity for her and said he could give her something to put on. My uncle was a clerk at Thorn's store, so he could afford to buy a blanket to give my mother to wear, and a small blanket for me and a little piece of one for the baby, Ntinti.

We all came then to Mafikeng, in the Roma Valley, where I still live today. The chief gave us an empty house, a rondavel, and my mother went to the Roman Catholics and they gave her work in the garden. So we started to have a little bit of clothes and we were eating *papa* like other people. But still no money. Sometimes we ate pumpkin seeds. People would give us the seeds when they ate the pumpkins. My mother would fry them and we would eat them with *papa*. The brother of my father laughed at us one day. He said, 'Your father is working in Gauteng, but he doesn't give your mother money. You eat what the mice eat.'

But at least we were eating. I didn't mind him.

17

When I remember that time I am puzzled, because it always seems to be a time of light. I know many times there were no candles in the house, no paraffin. But even when there were no candles, no paraffin, we made a fire at night and it seemed like there was a moon inside the house, there was so much light. I wonder if it was my mother's prayers that made such beautiful light in the dark house. Or maybe it was her singing. She said she tried to sing the hunger away.

There were no school fees at that time, and no uniforms. So that was when I started going to school. I went only in my little *thethana* (string skirt) and blanket. I was very happy to go to school. My mind was hungry for school in the same way my body was hungry for food. Already things were much better, and then came the biggest surprise of all.

In September 1938 my father sent money to my mother and said, 'You should come to me. Leave Sephefu and Ntinti with my mother at Mokhokhong. You come with the girl only.' So we went.

When we arrived in Gauteng my father was very glad, but was ashamed when he looked at my mother, and he cried to see her. A grown man, standing in the station, he was crying. My mother asked, 'Why do you cry?'

He told us this story. 'I cry because I had a dream that came three times. I saw a woman passing with a baby on her back, and this woman was crying. There were streaks on her face where the tears fell. And I heard a voice, it said, "Johannes, Johannes, who is passing there?"'

'I say, "It's Valeria."'

'Then the voice says, "Did you find her like that?"'

'And I wake up. I take a few days. The dream comes again. This time the voice is very loud. It says again, "Johannes, Johannes, who is passing?" and I say, "*Ke* Valeria," and the voice is gone.

'The third time the dream came, it was a voice both loud and hard. I don't know what kind of voice, if it is a man's voice or a woman's. This third time it shouts at me, "Johannes, Johannes, who is that lady wearing a sack with a baby on her back?" This time I don't answer. I just wake up. I sit on my chair, and the lady who is living with me says, "*Hao, Ntate* Johannes, why do you sit on the chair? It's time for sleep now."

'I cannot answer. I am just crying, leaving my head on the table. It feels too heavy with sadness even to lift it up. The lady asks me, "Why are you crying?"

'I say, "Don't ask me. I'm afraid to say. But this is the third time I dream this dream."

'"What kind of dream?"

'"Oh, my wife, my wife and children."

'"Your wife? Have you got a wife and children? Since I have been staying with you, you never told me that. I wonder how is this woman eating and what is she wearing?"

'I say, "No. Don't talk like that. You make me see this picture again, from my dream. My wife is wearing a sack and crying."

'"I am afraid of you, *Ntate* Johannes. You are not good to me, that I live here all this time and you never tell me you have a wife who is waiting for money and receiving nothing. When your wife comes here we must not be together. I'm going to look for another place to live. I'm ashamed to see your wife. You have treated your wife like a dog."

'I say to her, "I hear what you say. In the morning I will take the money and go post to my wife. I can't sleep any more."'

So my father told us that before 8 a.m., he was at the post office waiting for it to open so that he could post this money to my mother.

The money arrives in Roma, and we go. We have to get a bus to Maseru, and then a train from Maseru to Bloemfontein; another train from Bloemfontein to Germiston. In the morning we arrive in Germiston, and from there we take another train to Benoni. There, when we arrive in Benoni Station at only half past eight, we are surprised to find my father standing on one leg, because he has lost one leg. My mother is very shocked by this. She didn't know. He is standing like a cock, waiting to see a person who is wearing a sack and has streaks down her face from the tears. My mother has streaks down her face, like in the dream, but she is wearing a big Basotho dress, wide and full, and a big headwrap, like the Maxhosa women wear, on her head. My father comes and greets us, and tells us this story of the three dreams while we are on the way to his house. We take a taxi to Benoni Location, and we find there many black people, some Indians we call *Makula*, and some coloureds. It is my first time to see so many different kinds of people. We are listening to the story and looking, looking at this new place, our home now.

When we arrive at his house, we find rice with meat. We didn't know what is rice. We have never seen it before. We think it is maggots, and we are afraid. *Ntate* says 'No, it's like *samp*.' He says he would not feed us maggots. But we push the pieces of rice around and we are worried. We eat the bread only, because we are afraid of the rice. But he teaches us, 'No, see – this is food.' And he eats some. We make faces at each other and we blink our eyes, we are disgusted. But he says, 'It's good. You must eat this. You will be healthy.'

Finally we say, 'Oh, *ke hantle*, OK, we didn't know.' And we eat. We find it tastes all right, but we still feel strange to put these round white things in our mouths.

All the time while we are eating my father sits and looks at my mother, staring at the marks on her face from her tears. She never wiped the tears away because she had no Vaseline at that time, and the salt from her tears made lines down her face. Streaks, like in his dream. I was used to see these marks, so I was not noticing them until I see my father looking and looking and crying.

So when we finish eating, and we have given greetings and told our stories and seen the house, *Ntate* takes us to the shop, the very same day when we arrive. There he buys us some new clothes, because he wants my mother to take off this old-fashioned long dress. She was proud of it, because it was her best dress and her only one, and it took her a long time to have a dress and not a sack. It was the way in Lesotho for ladies to wear these long dresses. The skirt was large, and it sat on many petticoats, so when my mother walked, it floated around her like the plumes of an ostrich. When she had to go in a taxi, the skirts had to be pushed through the door.

But my father said it was an embarrassment to him. People in South Africa did not dress in this way. My father was staying in South Africa for a long time, and many people thought he was a

Zulu. He liked this, and he didn't want people to see that his wife came from Lesotho. So my mother took off two of her four petticoats, but she would not take them all off, because she thought if she took them all off, she would look like a man. At that time it was bad for a woman to look like a man; it would mean she was a woman who didn't take care of herself. My father bought cloth for my mother to make a new dress with, one that had a skirt only down to the knees, like other women in South Africa; and a blouse and shoes. He bought two dresses for me, and shoes with socks. And we went back home.

I was like a person in a dream. I had new food, new clothes, many things I never saw before. I was happy to see this new life for me and my mother, because I was always wondering if my mother told the truth when she said I've got a father. I asked, 'But if I have a father, why don't we have nice things for Easter and Christmas, like other children who have fathers?' Easter was a very big day at that time, especially if you have a husband or a father. Everything will be new. We will see a person in church wearing these nice new things, and we will say, 'Her father is working in Gauteng.'

So I feel amazed when I see this happens to me. I think, 'If I was in Lesotho they would see me like other girls who have fathers. They would see me in my new dress and shoes.' I thought I would like to fly like a bird and be in Lesotho again to show the people my new things. I would show them and think, 'You used to laugh at me and my mother, but look at us now.' In time, my mother had a chance to go back and show them. She took the trains back to Maseru and the bus back to the Roma Valley, leaving me in Benoni because she was not going to stay long in Lesotho.

She told me what happened. She said that when she went to church in her nice clothes, her skin all healthy and oiled, she was looking more beautiful than anyone in Roma ever saw her look before. The Chief's wife, the one who used to give my mother a handful of mealie kernels when my mother ground meal for her all day, she saw my mother going up for Holy Communion and she shouted, '*Hei!*' out loud, in the church.

People looked all around.

'*Hei!*' she shouts again, and again out loud she says, 'Is this Valeria?' The people all turn around and see my mother wearing a heavy skirt for winter, very fashionable like they wear in Gauteng, and two small blankets around her shoulders. One was maroon and one was blue, and she tied them together nicely and had a big *doek* on her head. So this lady says, '*Hei!* Is it Valeria, this one?'

The people look at her. Look at her. When the church is out, the Chief's wife was shy even to greet my mother, because she never thought my mother would look like that. So my mother greeted the Chief's wife warmly, and the people say, 'There is no poor person on earth who cannot be changed if only they have some money. Look at Valeria, how much a lady she is now, and how pretty.' They see that when you are poor and you have no food, you cannot help being ugly. Your skin looks tired and your diet is bad, so there is no shining on the skin but only dullness. It is also because your heart is always sad and you have no peace, so there is no shining from the inside either. You would like to be healthy and smiling like others, and you try to hold up your head and be grateful to be alive, but you are troubled in many ways and you cannot be beautiful. Yet if you have a little money, and you eat well, you can have an ugly face but no one will see that it is ugly. If there is peace in you, and health, you look beautiful.

CHAPTER 5

The High Court of Johannesburg

Most of the time between 1938 and 1948 my life was very good. I was living in Benoni with my mother and father. My mother was working in a factory, sewing sacks for coal and wood. My father was knitting. It was his work, and he taught my mother to knit and to sew with him. Since he had only one leg there was nothing else for him to do; but he was very good at knitting. He made hats and belts for schoolchildren, mostly. He and my mother were kind to each other, laughing and talking together.

Their work gave us enough money for us to live well, and I never saw them quarrel. We were living in a nice concrete-block house with a corrugated zinc roof, and we had other houses beside our house which we let other people rent. Benoni Location was very crowded. There were many houses so close together you could hear people talking on every side. The white people's town was half an hour away by bus. But the best thing about Benoni was the school. I liked school very much, until the time of the trouble between the black teacher and the white priest.

I went to St. Joseph's school, where we had black people of all nations: Zulu, Xhosa, Sotho, Tswana, and even coloureds. The teachers were all black people. I remember especially *Ntate* Makuta. He was very harsh. He beat us. When I was sitting in the school doing nothing and others were talking, he'd shout, 'Who is talking?'

Others would say, 'Mpho was talking,' and he would beat me. I wouldn't even cry. The children were jealous of me because I was smart. I knew the Catechism very well, because I learned it in Lesotho before I went to Benoni. When teachers would ask me the Catechism, I could answer every question, didn't even have to think about it first.

But the other children would say, 'This Mosotho thinks she's smart. Thinks she is better than anybody else.' They talked about me in Zulu and Xhosa and thought I couldn't understand them. But I did, and I knew they were jealous.

I told my father, and he was angry. He went to the school and shouted at the teachers, 'Every day this child comes home and tells me you don't like her. I don't see her exams because you don't give them to her to bring home. I want to see her papers, please.'

They didn't want to show him. I don't know why. He said, 'If you don't give me her exam papers I will go to the Principal and tell him.' The teachers were afraid of the Principal. My father saw the papers and saw that they were very good. So my father went to Father Gilbert, the white priest of the mission.

Next day Father Gilbert came to our classroom and asked *Ntate* Makuta, 'Why is it that the children don't like Mpho?'

Ntate Makuta said, 'I don't know.' Father Gilbert looked at him, and *Ntate* Makuta said, 'Maybe it is because this child is clever, and they are jealous.'

Father Gilbert said, 'She must go to another class. These children don't like her, and they make her life hard. I think she can do the work of another class, where the children will not be so far behind her and where they won't be jealous.'

So I got a new teacher. The new teacher asked me the Catechism, and I knew it well, and there were others in that class who knew it well, so they were not so jealous. From there I went to school like other people, all the way to Standard Six. I liked to study English and Afrikaans, Zulu and Xhosa. Now sometimes I mix up Zulu and Tswana, but then I knew them all very well, because in school I was playing with other children, and I wanted to speak each language. The teachers liked to work with us in many languages, too. One day the teacher would say, 'Today we will do all of our lessons in Tswana only.' Or another day, Afrikaans. Or Sesotho. It was very good practice for us, and the teachers helped us to know the grammar for each language. We were students of many nations, and we never had trouble between us like they do now, in Gauteng. We were never fighting in groups. The only time we had trouble was when we were walking to school and we passed by the location where the coloured people lived, and they would throw stones at us. When we passed there, every day we had to choose: do we run, or do we fight with them? But all of us in my school were together, and we never fought with each other. Then came the fight between Father Gilbert and *Ntate* Makuta.

Father Gilbert always liked to come in the classrooms and ask us the Catechism. Sometimes he came without asking permission. Most of the teachers didn't mind about this. They just waited a while, and when Father Gilbert was finished, they went on like before. But *Ntate* Makuta didn't like this interruption, totally. He wanted to go on with his lessons, not be stopped by Father Gilbert coming to ask Catechism. He told Father Gilbert to go away.

So one day when I was in Standard Six we had to go to class with *Ntate* Makuta. He was being nasty the way he always was, and I know he still hated me from before, and I was not happy in the class, but I did the work like everybody else. Again Father Gilbert came, trying to ask the Catechism, and *Ntate* Makuta told him to go away.

Father Gilbert says, 'Every day when I come to ask the Catechism, you tell me to go away. You always say I must get out of your class.'

Ntate Makuta says, 'Yes, I don't want you here.' He never liked Father Gilbert.

Father Gilbert says, 'This is my school, too, and I have a job here, which is to ask the Catechism. I can't go out.'

Suddenly *Ntate* Makuta hits Father Gilbert with his fist. He hits him with his fist in the face, and he grabs Father Gilbert's clothes with his hand, and he shakes Father Gilbert and hits him. Father Gilbert doesn't hit back, he just tries to break free and get away, but *Ntate* Makuta holds onto him.

We start to scream in the classroom, trying to stop *Ntate* Makuta. Another teacher comes from next door and tries to get Father Gilbert loose from *Ntate* Makuta before *Ntate* can kill him. Blood is coming out of Father Gilbert's nose. Another teacher comes, and finally they make *Ntate* Makuta let go of Father Gilbert. He has to go wash his face because it's bleeding so much. After washing, Father Gilbert takes his car and goes to Benoni Court to make papers against *Ntate* Makuta.

Father Gilbert comes back to the school and says he wants me to be his witness. I was in the classroom when the fight happened, and Father Gilbert remembered me from when I had trouble with *Ntate* Makuta and he helped me to get into another teacher's class, so Father Gilbert says I have to come to the High Court, in Johannesburg. I was very much afraid. Father Gilbert says, 'You must tell the truth, my child. Just tell what happened.'

Before we go to the court, *Ntate* Makuta comes to me and says I must not tell about the fight. I must say I can't remember what happened. He says he knows I love Father Gilbert, but this time I must not tell the truth, because I must be loyal to my people. I go to the court, and while I am going there I don't know what I will say.

We come to the High Court in Johannesburg. I look at the Judge. He is a big white man in a black robe and a white wig, and he is very quiet and angry. Other children from the school are in the courtroom, listening, but I am the only one who is going to be a witness. So I am asked by the court, what did I see. There was a translator – we call him a *toloko* – in case I can't understand English. But I understand what they ask me. They say, 'What did you see?'

Suddenly I feel like somebody poured a bucket of water over my head. The whole of my body is cold, and then hot. I take a long time, it feels like ten minutes, waiting. I can't speak. I am praying in my heart, 'God, help me.'

They say, 'You must speak!'

I tell the truth. I tell them I saw *Ntate* Makuta hit Father Gilbert in the face.

They say, 'How did *Ntate* Makuta hit Father Gilbert?'

I say, 'He hit him with his fist, and he grabbed his clothes with his other hand and held him so he could hit him again.'

So the High Court decided *Ntate* Makuta had to pay some money to Father Gilbert, and *Ntate* had to take a few months to go away from the school. Later *Ntate* Makuta moved to Orlando Location. I knew he hated me for telling the truth in that Court. I didn't even tell the truth because I loved Father Gilbert, but because I was afraid of that Judge. He is the one who said I had to tell the truth. He said, 'Tell us exactly what you saw.' You should only see the face of this Judge, and you would tell the truth too. I was sixteen at that time, and after the day in court, I went back to school. I stayed in school until the day I was married.

CHAPTER 6

Two Marriages, One Husband

One Sunday when I was eighteen, I was sitting in church with ribbons in my hair like a crown. I was thinking about Lesotho, trying to remember. I thought about the hunger and the beauty of the place. My mother took me from there in 1938, because of a dream that came three times. Now it was 1948, and I was sitting in church, but I did not hear the prayers at all. I was tired of living in Benoni Location, and I was beginning to be homesick.

A Mosotho miner who was also living in Benoni saw me in church that day. He asked a girl who was a friend of mine, 'Is this a Mosotho girl?'

My friend sees that this miner is interested in me, and she says, 'Yes. She is living in Benoni Location with her parents, in Number 32 on Fourth Street. You can find her there.' That was the beginning, and I came to love Alexis Nthunya before his family kidnapped me and forced us to marry.

Right there outside the church in Benoni, the first time he ever saw me, Alexis said to my friend, 'I love this Mpho. I want to marry her.'

'I don't know,' my friend said to him. 'Her father is very fierce, very *bohale*. He won't have any nonsense with his child.'

My friend came to me later and told me what happened. I told her I wanted to see that gentleman. I wanted to see who loved me and wanted to marry me, when he never even spoke to me. So she told me she would ask him to come to church the next Sunday to meet me.

So we go. After church the girl calls to me and says, 'Here is Alexis Nthunya, the gentleman I was talking about. He says he loves you and he wants to marry you.'

I say, '*Hei!* I don't want to be married.'

She says, 'Why? You want to stay in Benoni so you can make children without fathers?'

I say, 'No. My mother will pray for me not to have children.' I don't say that I am tired of Benoni. I just watch Alexis and see how he looks at me.

He says, 'I want to take this Mosotho girl back to Lesotho, because I see she is a good child. I want to take her home.'

I began to fall in love with this man. He was very handsome; all the girls who saw him wanted him. He was medium-brown complexion, with a big nose; large, soft lips; and huge, round eyes. He was tall and muscular, and he loved to dress well. He always wanted to wear peg-legged pants, and when he was riding a horse, with his blanket over his shoulders, he looked like a chief. Whenever he went anywhere dressed up, on his horse, people would bow to him and call him *Morena*, Chief.

We met many times, always at church on Sunday because I could not see him any other time. My father was very strict; if he saw me standing with a boy he would hit me like a dog. So I just met Alexis in church, but he was always very nice, and he always looked at me in that way, and I began to fall in love with him. He was a quiet man, and gentle. Not like many others. I saw he was a good man.

When Alexis went to the mines he wrote me letters in Sesotho, and I wrote back to him. One day my father found a letter and said, 'Where does this letter come from?'

I said, ' I don't know.'

My father took the letter and said he would tear it up, and I went to find my friend who introduced me to Alexis. I told her my father has this letter and I knew he was going to beat me. This young woman went to my father and said, '*Ntate*, this child is big enough. She must have boyfriends. How can she marry without knowing any boys at all? There is one Mosotho boy from the mines; he wants to marry her, so he wrote the letter, speaking about love. So don't tear the letters, and don't beat her. She is big enough to have a boyfriend.'

Ntate says, 'OK, because you have told me this, I will leave the letters. From where does this gentleman come?' And we talk.

He asks me, 'Where does this man see you?'

I say, 'In the church only.'

He says, 'He must be a good man. He goes to church. You are talking with him about love?'

I say 'Yes'.

He says, 'Where is his home? Who is his family?'

I say, 'His home is Marakabei, District of Maseru, in the Maluti mountains. His name is Nthunya.'

My father thinks about this. He looks away for a long time, and then he says, 'Yes, he must be a good gentleman. You must not take any *tsotsis* for boyfriends.'

I say 'Yes, father.' This is in 1948.

Some time later my father got a letter from the parents of Alexis. They asked for me. They said, 'Our son wants to marry your daughter, Mpho.'

So my father asks me again, 'Do you know Alexis Moalosi Nthunya? Do you?'

I say, 'Yes, *Ntate*. He is the Mosotho I told you about, the one I met in church, who writes me letters from the mines, speaking about love.'

'Yes,' my father says. 'Here is a letter from his parents. They want you to marry their son, and they will pay nice *lobola*, bride-price, for you.'

So it was decided. My mother and I came to Lesotho to receive the *lobola*, and I went to school at St. Mary's to learn hand-sewing, so I could be a good wife. My *lobola* was nine cows, twelve goats, and one horse, and we had to find people to look after those animals in Roma, Lesotho, which was our real home. I enjoyed learning to sew and getting ready for my marriage. I made myself two dresses of the small-print cloth Basotho women like to wear – we call it *seshoeshoe* because it is a cloth of Basotho women, even though it is made in England. Then we took my new dresses, packed them, and went back to Gauteng to make more clothes for me and a white dress for the church wedding.

Early in the morning on the day after my mother and I came back from Lesotho, I was sitting at the table trying to write a letter to Alexis, because I wanted him to know I was back in Benoni. I heard a child say, '*Ausi* Mpho, two ladies are calling you outside.'

I leave my pen and writing pad on the table and go find the two ladies at the gate. They say, '*Ausi*, come with us halfway to the shops, there. Your gentleman wants to talk to you.'

I say, 'Who?'

'Alexis Nthunya wants to talk to you. He heard that you were back here.'

We go. We get to the first store. We don't find him. A lady in the store says, 'No, he says he will be there, in Tenth Street.' We are in Fifth Street.

We go. When we arrive there, nobody. Another lady says, 'Oh, maybe he was here but he sees that you are late. He must go to work in the afternoon. Maybe he's at that house close by.'

She points to the house, and one of the two ladies with me says, 'Let's go quickly, because I'm afraid of Mpho's father, if he finds us.'

When we go to that house, we knock. A lady says, 'Come in.'

There are two men: my gentleman, Alexis, and an old man. I greet them. They answer me, and the lady of the house gives me a chair and says, 'Sit down and talk quickly, because I'm afraid of Mpho's father.'

Alexis says, politely, '*E-a, 'M'e*' (Yes, Ma'am).

We talk. He asks me about Lesotho, and how many cows did his father bring for *lobola* to my house. I tell him nine cows, twelve goats, and one horse. He asks me now, why did we come to Benoni again, after the *lobola* is paid. I say, 'I'm coming to buy some clothes for marriage.'

He says, 'Oh, I understand. Because even myself, I want to have nice clothes for marriage. So you are going to buy a white dress?'

I say, 'Yes, a white dress. I want a white dress for my marriage.' And we speak of many things.

But suddenly the time is gone, because since I arrived I see three hours have passed. I am surprised when that lady comes again and says, 'Mpho, you are not going anywhere from now.'

'*Hao, 'M'e!*' I ask her why. I say, 'I must go home. My parents will worry.'

She says, 'No. You have been paid *lobola*, but your parents brought you to Benoni again, where the *tsotsis* will come and take you. So we don't want our cows and goats and horse to go up and down for nothing. You are no more going out of this house.'

I say I'm going out.

She says, 'So we shall see. You can't.' And she looks at Alexis and says, 'You didn't tell this girl that there is no more going out?'

He says, 'I'm afraid to tell her,' and I know it is because he loves me and doesn't want me to be afraid.

And she answers Alexis, 'I'm not playing with you. It's true, she can't go out. My father brought cows and goats and a horse to her family in Lesotho. After that, her parents brought her here again. They have the cows. They should leave her in Lesotho to wait for you. No. You must tell her she is your wife, and she is not going out. If you are afraid to tell her, I will tell her.'

Alexis and I feel shy, then. So the lady goes in another room and takes a new blanket and puts it on my shoulders. I throw it off.

She says, 'It's a pity, because you are going to put it on. You are not going out, totally.' So she goes out and my gentleman is now very scared and frightened. He does not want me to be unhappy or afraid, but his sister is quarrelling with him.

I say, 'Why do you do this to me?'

He says, 'It's not me. It is my sister, 'M'athuso, who does this. I'm ashamed, because your father is looking for you now. We waste time by sitting here, but now I don't know what I can do, because now you have been given the blanket. We are married.'

I say, 'I'm going out.'

But the lady has locked the door and the windows. She says, 'This girl is a *tsotsi*. She will fly. I am taking the key. I am locking the windows.'

She goes away and finds the headman in that part of the location. We call him the Chief, or *induna*. She comes back with this Chief and he asks me, 'What is your name?'

I tell him.

'What is your father's name?'

I say, 'Johannes Lillane, from Fourth Street, Number 32.'

He writes it down and he says, 'You know this gentleman?'
I say, 'Yes.'
'Did you ever talk about marriage?'
I say, 'Yes.'
'He has given *lobola* to your father's house in Lesotho?'
I say, 'Yes.'
Then he says, 'Look here, this gentleman is your husband from now, my dear, because he has given *lobola* to your family, and his family has given you the new blanket. So the relatives of this gentleman say they don't want you to be taken away by the *tsotsis* here. The *tsotsis* like to take pretty women your age and put them to work. But remember those cows, goats, and horse. You must not worry from now. Sit down, my dear, and know that this is your husband. I am going now to your house and tell your father not to worry because your husband has taken you home.'

It was now late, because I was seeing children passing from school as I was looking out the window. So I stayed there, doing nothing but talking to my gentleman. He was shy because he didn't like what his sister was doing, quarrelling with him in front of me. At five o'clock he was supposed to go to work, so then I was left with the ladies. I was worried because of my mother and father. I was not feeling all right, and I did not sleep well.

Early in the morning, about six, the Chief came back and said he has been to my parents. 'The mother of the girl says she is glad to learn the girl is here, because she was worried. She was afraid the *tsotsis* had taken her, and she could not see how she could give back the cows and the goats and the horse. But she says you must bring her back to go to church for the marriage.' Then the Chief went away.

Right then the brother of the ladies went and got one sheep. He brought it back to the house where I was staying and made it stand by the door. They said, 'Come and see your food. We have a sheep.'

I looked, and I went back and sat down. The ladies were sewing a new dress for me to wear, a gray one of *seshoeshoe*. After they sewed it, they dressed me in it. The men were killing the sheep, and they took two ribs and put them on the fire and then gave to me to eat. So from that day, they told me, 'You are married. Alexis is your husband.'

I ate the ribs, and my husband's family ate the sheep, and we had *papa*. I was feeling better, because I knew my parents were not worried any more, but I wanted to go back for a church marriage. I began to talk to them, to work in the house with the new gray dress on, and it was no more feeling bad.

Because Alexis was working night shift we could not be together at night during that week, so it was not until Saturday that we shared the blanket. His sister told me what would happen when we shared the blanket, because I did not know these things.

We had a room with a bed, and when we shared the blanket it made much blood. When I woke up in the morning, his sister came for the sheets to be sure there was blood, so she would know it was my first time to share the blankets. She took the sheets away.

I said, 'Why do you take these sheets? I am embarrassed. I was going to wash them.'

But she says, 'No. I'll wash them,' and she looks pleased.

Sunday Alexis and I were together again, and on Monday he went to work the night shift. I did not like sharing the blanket because it was my first time to do it, and it hurt. In the morning when you wake up, you feel shy when you see the other people. You know they are looking at you and knowing what happened.

I stayed there eight months without going out, until Christmas holidays. I never went to my parents' home from that day. My mother was just seeing me in the church; my father too. They asked if I was feeling all right. I said I was all right, no complaints. And from there, in December, Alexis took me to Marakabei, where my baby came and died in April.

Finally after I was finished doing all the proper Sesotho things about that baby, I went to my mother and father, who have moved back home to Roma, and we prepared for my church marriage. It came on a Wednesday. The priest was *Ntate* Lelimo, a Mosotho Christian priest. We were staying with my mother, and we woke very early to go to the church. I took two other girls, one as my witness and another one who was my friend; and Alexis came with three men, a witness and two friends. All of my mother's family came, but only one man from Alexis's family and one other from his village could come.

I really wanted this church marriage because I could not take Holy Communion if I was married out of the church. This made me worried the whole year, but even worse than that, my mother could not take Holy Communion because of me. My mother did not like to stay without Holy Communion, so I was sorry for her and I felt ashamed. When the priest was reading the marriage I was not listening to the words. I was feeling much love for Alexis and for my mother, so I was very happy. I could not wear a white dress because I already had a baby, so I was wearing just a new dress and a cap, and new shoes. My mother went to Benoni and bought these clothes before I had the baby, and she saved them for me.

So after the church marriage we went home with these people, our witnesses and friends, and my mother's family, and there was much *joala* for everyone who wanted it. Many people were outside sitting, waiting for *joala* and food, before we even got back from the church. My mother and father slaughtered a sheep and made a feast for all the people who were there. I stayed inside the house, not with the people outside. I was not drinking *joala*, I was drinking ginger ale. But Alexis wanted *joala*, so they had plenty.

In the morning, maybe 3 a.m., before light, we have to go. Nobody must see us, it's a tradition. We didn't sleep totally. We go riding horses, because Alexis and his brother brought horses for themselves and for me. We go with a new suitcase full of clothes my mother prepared for me, along with dishes and brooms and many things. (These things were not dear at that time. A dress was fifteen cents.) We slept on the way, in Makhaleng.

Early the next morning we woke up, but not at 3 a.m. We saddled the horses and went again. At 6 o'clock that night we arrived home. We were very tired, so when we arrived, we found some *joala* again – another big feast of *joala* and meat. People came again and drank, and ate meat with *papa*. People brought small presents, like brooms made of grass, mugs and jugs, plates. Not many presents, because the people are poor there, but they brought what they could. I was very glad to get home again with my new clothes, and on Sunday I went to church and took Holy Communion.

CHAPTER 7

South African Police

The Boer policemen are like a nightmare to me: a picture which moves, always the same. I can see it if my eyes are open or if they are shut. I see them in their black suits with yellow shining things on the neck, a black hat with a yellow patch, and black boots. White, white skin and red eyes like white rats. They carry short sticks. When they beat people on the head with these sticks, the sticks are very heavy. I am afraid of them.

The police were many in Benoni Location. One time the police were arresting a Mosotho, and we knew the police were going to kill him. This man's brothers fought with the police and killed one of the white policemen with their *molamu* and an axe with a long handle, we call it a *koakoa*. When they cut the policeman's head off, his head bounced away in one direction like a ball, his body in another direction. We knew there would be trouble after.

After the Basotho killed this policeman, other policemen came from other places; they were called to come and kill the Basotho. There were many Boers now, with guns and tear-gas, and the white policemen called many *Maxhosa* to help them, and they put the *Maxhosa* in front, so it was like an army of *Maxhosa* making war against the Basotho in the streets outside their own homes, with the Boers coming behind with guns. The tear-gas was there, so the Basotho ran away and the *Maxhosa* and Boers chased after them. Many people died, white and *Maxhosa*. Only four Basotho died. Others had to go to the hospitals.

The Boers didn't like to fight the Basotho; they sent the *Maxhosa* to fight us so it would be only black people dying. I think the Boers still use black people to fight black people; it is their way, because the black people always are poor and need

37

money, so the Boers can buy them. It is easy to buy people whose children are hungry. They will do anything to feed their children.

The first time I saw the policemen in Gauteng, they were catching black people and putting them in a car, kicking them and forcing them to jail. That was when I was in Benoni with Alexis right after my marriage. They came to the house where we slept. They knocked hard on the door, and they shouted at us, '*Vula! Vula!* Open! Open!'

Then the owner of the house, who was Alexis's cousin, went and opened the door.

They say, 'Permits! We want permits!'

And they checked to see if every person in the house has a permit.

I didn't have a permit because it was only right after Alexis's family took me to make me his wife. I was maybe four or five days living in that house, so when they find this, they say, '*Phuma! Hamba!*' Which we can see means I should go out. I go.

Alexis was not there; he was working. I go with them to the car. We were full in that car – it was like a combi, they called it a 'pick-up' because the police use it to pick up many people and take them to jail. We go to the police station. We were just like sheep there. They shout at us, 'Come on, come on!' So I got very frightened because I didn't like those policemen and I didn't know what they would do to me. This is why I still have nightmares about them. If I see them I am so much afraid I start to shake inside, like when it is very cold. It can be summer and I still feel this cold.

'Get in!' They push me in the jail, with many other women. I stay there for two days. All the other women were there because they didn't have permits or they were caught selling *joala*.

They feed us *papa* with salt on it. Tea to drink with small sugar, very little sugar. It was a big room with a bucket at one end for using the toilet. You go there and relieve yourself and there is nothing to wipe with. And you have to eat in the same room with this bucket which everyone in the room has to use. Blankets on the floor – black blankets, very dirty. Some of the women said there were fleas, but I didn't see them.

After two days there came a white policeman. He stands just at the door, looks in and shouts, '*Gaan uit*! Come on!'

We don't know who he means to come on. He is just standing at the door staring at us. We are sitting. Nobody moves. It seems like nobody is breathing in this room. He doesn't call the name of a person. We wait.

Then the policeman comes, opens the door to the cell, and says to me, 'Agnes! Come out!' So I come out. I don't know if maybe they are going to kill me, or what.

I find my husband outside. I sign the papers and I go; we go home. Alexis had to pay them twenty pounds. That was very much money back then. He took the money he was making from work, and he paid them. After that, I got a permit. It's like a passport, a permit to stay in that house. I didn't have one because I was not staying in that house – my permit was for my parents' house. You have to have a permit to sleep in a particular house.

They could come any time they like, come to the Location and get people – maybe men, maybe women – and beat them, shove them in the pick-up, yell at them like they yell at dogs. They can do horrible things I cannot even speak about.

Even now, I know these white policemen still kill people in the Republic. We always hear that they are still killing men in the mines. When it's a fight in the mines, and the Boer police come in, they come not to make peace but to beat or to kill as many black men as they can. People say they smile when they are hitting the black men. It gives them pleasure.

When they look at you with their red eyes, it's frightening. They are jealous, always jealous of the black people. I don't know why. They don't like black people. I think about why, but I can't find any answer. They just hate us. They call us monkeys.

The second time I went to Benoni, after the first two babies died, I had a permit, everything I needed to have. I saw them passing through the streets, looking for illegal *joala*. People would dig holes in the ground and put a tank of *joala* in it, then cover it up and smear it so it looks like the floor. Put a mat over it, and nobody can know there is *joala* in this house.

When the police go in a house they take sharp sticks and they pound the floor with these sticks, looking. They break the woman's things, tear her mats, make holes in her linoleum. If they find a hidden tank of *joala*, they say 'Take this out of the ground.'

She takes it out and they put her in the pick-up. If they like, they will take the *joala* with her. Sometimes they pour the *joala* all over the house and say, 'Go in the pick-up with your empty tank.'

I was never making *joala* when I lived in Gauteng, but still the police would come and make holes in my mats with their sticks, looking for *joala*. When they are in my house I am shaking, shaking like a herdboy in winter, even if it is a hot day. They can do anything they like with you. Even now it is so.

After this I tell Alexis I want to come home to Lesotho, because I don't want to see these things. So we come home to Marakabei, but I still have nightmares about these policemen. I don't want them, with their red eyes. I don't know why they have these red eyes. Maybe it's the hate in them.

CHAPTER 8

The Land of the Wild Sage

In midsummer, right after Christmas, Alexis took me home to the Maluti Mountains of Lesotho. We packed all our clothes and left the dust, noise, Boer police, and constant fighting of Benoni Location, where Alexis and I had been forced to live as husband and wife since Easter. And we went to Marakabei, my new home.

I didn't know anything about Marakabei and those Maluti Mountains. I saw little hills, we called them mountains, when I was a small child living in Lesotho, near Roma. But always the hills were at a distance. I did not know the size of them. Alexis said the Maluti were very different from the hills of Roma; he said I could not imagine them, and it was true. I was wanting to see my new home and family, and these mountains Alexis told me about, but I was not happy on the way, because I was tired. I tried not to grumble.

We took the trains to Maseru; from Maseru a bus to Roma; and from Roma we had to walk by foot to Makhaleng, which is half the way from Roma to Marakabei. I was four months pregnant with the child who was going to die, and I carried a brown suitcase with clothes for me and Alexis, and Alexis carried a gray bag with more clothes. My feet were tired, tired. We found some people in Makhaleng who let us sleep at their house. They were friends of Alexis, and they gave us food and let us sleep on the floor on sheepskins.

The next day we woke up and began to walk again. We walked the whole day by foot, uphill most of the time, around steep cliffs and winding paths. I began to see what mountains are, but still I did not see mountains like those in Marakabei. When it was late afternoon, the postman passed us on horseback, with an extra horse carrying some mail. Alexis asked the man, 'Please, can you

41

put this lady on the one horse? We are going to Marakabei, but she is tired now. It's the first time for her to walk like this, such a great distance.' So the postman put me on the horse carrying the mail. This was also my first time to ride a horse, but because I was tired, I didn't even care enough to be afraid I would fall off. Then we go. Alexis is walking by foot, but the postman and I go on ahead of him. Soon the postman has to go a different way, so he leaves me in a small village and says to the ladies, 'Please take care of this person. Her husband is coming. She will stay here and the man will come and collect her.'

The ladies gave me some *papa* and some *mafi* (sour milk) to eat with it. I was glad to have something to eat. But it was now sunset, and no Alexis. Just as the sun was down, Alexis came running, running very fast and found me. He says, 'Marakabei is still a distance away.'

We walk on in the dark, stumbling sometimes over the stones, carrying our suitcase and our bag. I keep on asking him, 'When are we going to arrive in this place?'

And he tells me he doesn't know when. He laughs, 'I told you this place is very far.' We were winding in and out between the hills, along a footpath, but I couldn't see what was around me in the dark. I couldn't see the mountains and the cliffsides, so I didn't even know how to be afraid. I smelled the sharp strong leaves of the wild sage that grows all over the Maluti. It was a new smell to me, a clean, wild smell, and I liked it.

Finally we find the house, a large rondavel and many people, Alexis's family. His mother and father are there, and his sisters and brothers, and many children, all wanting to see the new wife of Alexis. We sit down. They give me *papa* and *mafi*, the same thing I ate with the ladies in the village on the way, and I say, 'No. I won't eat it.'

They say, 'What are we going to do now? It is too late to cook sheep.' But their father tells them to bring the sheep.

I say, 'Thank you,' and sit down.

They bring the sheep, show it to me, and kill it quickly. They take the liver and two ribs and put them on the fire and give to me to eat. I eat them with the *papa*. They say, 'Oh, maybe she wants tea. They drink much tea in Gauteng, where this Mosotho girl has been living a long time.' But there is no tea in that house.

They offer me the drink they make from sorghum, a sour porridge we call *motoho*. I say, 'No, I don't eat sour porridge, because it hurts my tonsils.'

They go up and down to other people's houses, looking for tea. I didn't know they had no tea there, or I could put some in my suitcase to bring with me. At first I thought they could go to the store to buy some, but they have no stores there. Only mountains. At last they find some tea, and I drink it. Alexis drinks *joala*. And we go to sleep.

The next day I woke up tired, so tired from walking all that way by foot. We slept in the rondavel on sheepskins, and I got up, looked out the door and saw the mountains. I sucked in my breath, 'Ah!' I was shocked to see them so near to my face, so big and close, larger than anything I have ever seen. Then I smiled inside myself, thinking, 'So this is the Maluti.'

The land was quiet, peaceful, and very pleasing to my eyes. I liked the colours, the shapes of the mountain-tops, the way the shadows from the clouds fall and move across the mountains so everything is always changing. Everywhere I could smell wild sage. I like the wild sage and clean mountain wind, the colours of the wildflowers: bright blue, deep yellow, or maybe red and orange like flames of the fire. I like the sounds, the birds and the crickets, the waterfall near the house, the music of sheep-bells and cow-bells, the silence. Most of all I like the silence. The people there are quiet. No fighting, no yelling, and there are no buses, no engines. You can see a few trucks or buses if you go to Marakabei village, which is far away, but it is so still, in the mountains there. Later in my time in the Maluti, sometimes an airplane would pass overhead, and I would wave to it and say, 'Fine, go on. You can have those towns you fly to. Say hello to my mother when you pass over her. I am happy to stay here.'

I saw that even though the mountains were strange to me, I was going to be at home in them. It was going to be good life for me. I took a bucket to go to fetch some water, but the path was steep and I didn't know it. I was looking over the edge of the path, afraid I would fall. The people at the stream laughed at me.

I said, 'What are you laughing at?'

They were laughing because I couldn't put the bucket on my head, because I was afraid to fall with it on the steep path. So they laughed. They said, '*Hei!* Alexis has wasted his cows on this woman. Is she a woman or a *lekhooa* (white person)?' They thought I was not going to stay in the Maluti, but they were wrong.

I laughed back at them in my heart. They didn't know how tired I was of the town. After only one morning, I knew I wanted to stay there in the mountains. The town had too many people, too much noise all the time, no peace. *Tsotsis*, gangsters were everywhere stealing things, fighting; other people always fighting. There was no peace totally. Basotho were fighting with Maxhosa; men were fighting with wives and girlfriends; men were drinking *joala* and fighting with anybody they see. Every day we saw some people dying in the streets, and when they were fighting, they didn't care whether you were fighting or not; when they found you on the way they could just kill you. I saw that the mountains were a better place, and I knew that I wanted to stay. But I had to learn many things.

When I came back from fetching the water, carrying the bucket in my hands like a white person, people were gathered to the house to come and see me. My mother-in-law chose a name for me and sent a friend of hers to tell me, 'Your new name is 'M'atsepo, which means Mother of Trust. We trust you, and so we give you this name.' I just looked at her, thinking about it. I didn't say anything. She said, 'You are supposed to say "Thank you" if you like the name.'

And I thanked her.

I was four months pregnant now at this time, but nobody could tell. I knew, and Alexis knew, but he didn't tell his mother when we arrived. After New Year, Alexis went back to Gauteng for work. I stayed there, living with his mother, who was called 'M'anthunya. She loved me very much, and I loved her. We were staying together, going to the fields together. In the fields we fetched maize for meal, or sorghum, which makes bread. We pulled off stalks and put the heads – we call them mealies – in sacks or big basins which we carried home on our heads.

There were two girls, one boy, *Ntate* Nthunya, 'M'anthunya, and me. *Ntate* was not working, just sitting, looking out over the mountains, thinking many things. If it's time to harvest, you must go to the fields, everyone except *Ntate*. 'M'anthunya would grind maize for meal, but I did not know how, because I came from Gauteng. I was a city girl. When they gave me the mealies, I said, 'I don't know what to do with these.'

They say, 'How is this possible? You have not been trained? Your father does not drink *motoho*? Oh, this child! They like to be married, but they don't know anything. This child is useless.'

I didn't care. I was laughing, and they were laughing too while they were grumbling. I was just like a fool. They were right, I didn't know how to do anything. So 'M'anthunya started to teach me. She gave me *mabele* (sorghum) and told me to grind it; she said it is softer than maize, it's a good way for me to learn grinding.

I laughed, and I said I couldn't do it.

His family says to Alexis, 'Where did you get this *lekhooa*, this white girl?'

He says, 'At Roma; from Roma to Benoni. She never used a grinding stone in her life. There was no grinding stone in her mother's house in Benoni.'

His mother asks, 'So why do you take this girl who knows nothing?'

'You will teach her. I did not marry her to come and fight with the stones here. I married her because I love her. She can come here and see what this life is like, and she can learn. Give her time. Give me the things to be ground and I will take them to the mill until she learns grinding.'

First 'M'anthunya taught me to make *joala*, because all the men like to drink it, and if I am a wife I must know this. She showed me the way while she did it. She said, 'You cook the water, and when it's boiling, you take the maize, put it in another pot, and take the boiling water and pour it in and stir it. Use a lot of water, and stir it long. Then you wait. When it's not hot, but just a little warm, you take a sour *motoho*, you put it in, just a little bit, so the whole mixture will come to be sour. Next day you cook this *lekoele*. After cooking it, you cool it. When it is cold, bring it together with *mela*, which is like meal. You heat it again. When it is good and sour, it's called *joala* and you put it through a sieve and it's done.'

Me, I don't like it. I never make it now. My mother, my father, and my brother didn't like it, and I didn't like it too. Many Basotho like to drink it too much, and it causes many problems. Sometimes when I was pregnant I would take just one glass when I was thirsty, but only one glass. They say it is good for pregnant women. But from there, no more.

So. I'm four months pregnant in December. The baby should come in May. I was busy learning many things from 'M'anthu-nya, and I didn't think much about the baby coming. I didn't know that the baby was going to come in April, a month early and too small to live.

When the summer came to an end and my time was closer for the baby, I began to be sick. I was not knowing what happened in my body. I was very tired and hot. Don't want to eat. Just drink. Basotho say a pregnant woman must not drink so much water; but I drink and drink. Can't get enough. Alexis came at the end of March to take me to see the doctor in Roma. We went on horses, but the trip was very difficult for me, and when we got to Dr Maema, he said I must go to hospital in Maseru. We thought he meant I should go home and get my things, and come back again to hospital to have the baby, and I knew that before I go to hospital for the baby, I must go first to my parents' home. We didn't understand that Dr Maema meant I should go now, now, at that very moment, to the hospital. We go back up to the mountains again.

In Lesotho when you are seven months pregnant with your first-born child, you go to your parents' house to do certain Sesotho things, to prepare properly. Your mother-in-law must say when it is time for you to go. My parents moved to Roma at the same time Alexis and I went to Marakabei – in December. We were living in Gauteng all those years because of my father's work, but he was tired, so they were going home to Lesotho when I went to the Maluti.

I was looking forward to seeing my parents again and preparing for the baby. But the way it happened, I did not see them until after the baby died, because my mother-in-law didn't know that I was pregnant, so she didn't send me to them at the right time. I was not counting the time. I thought Alexis told 'M'anthunya, and so I thought it was not my business to ask her when I was supposed to go back to my mother's house, so I said nothing.

When we return from seeing the doctor, we tell 'M'anthunya that I must go to hospital now, and she is surprised. She asks Alexis, 'How many months is your wife, when you say the doctor needs her to go to hospital?'

He says 'Eight.'

She says, 'Oh, why didn't you tell me in December when you arrived here that your wife is pregnant? She was supposed to go to her home at seven months and do the proper things.'

'What things?' we ask, because we don't know about these things. I know I am supposed to go, but I don't know for what.

'She must put on a little skirt which is only for pregnant women to wear, and a small shirt made of flannelette material with little cap-sleeves, called a *selapa*. Then she puts a red clay on her face, removes her shoes and her head-covering, and waits until the child comes. There are some other things that help her to get ready. Then, when the child comes she takes the *selapa* off her shoulders and wraps the child in it. But now it is too late, so what are we going to do?'

Alexis says, 'I don't know, 'M'e. I didn't know you wouldn't ask 'M'atsepo. I thought you would notice she is pregnant.'

She says, 'I didn't see she was pregnant because she has no stomach. She is so small. Now we have missed something which should be done at seven months. This is not good.'

I was sick, and I came to be sicker. I could not travel to go back to the hospital, which was in Maseru. There was a bus from Roma to Maseru, but the only way to get to Roma was by horse, and I couldn't stay on a horse. It was too painful. And in just five days from the time we got home, the child came.

'M'anthunya helped me to bring the baby out, with another lady. But when the baby came, she was tired, and they told me she was not going to live. She passed away after only one day. It was 1950, April. It was my first-born, a girl. And I was such a fool, I was not even sad. I never held my child, because she was sick from the time she was born, and I too was very sick. My stomach hurt, and it was hot. The baby was small, so I was not too sore where she came out, but I was very tired and weak. The thirst went away, and I was hungry, but when I ate I would vomit.

When the baby died, she was taken to *thotobolo*, the rubbish heap. They put the baby in a hole there in the rubbish heap. Only women could touch this dead baby that I never touched myself.

All this time Alexis was in town drinking *joala*. He knew I was sick, and after the baby came they told him the baby passed away. He was sad. It was only me, the fool, who was not sad. After about ten days I began to feel better, and I felt I must get up and work.

They cut my hair and put a white scarf on my head, we call it a *tubu*. I have to wear this white *tubu* for a whole month. After that month I have to go to my mother's house and leave the *tubu* and my old clothes there. My mother has to buy me new clothes. I stay with my mother only one week. Then I go back to the mountains. I would like to stay longer with my mother, but I was not supposed to, because I was not visiting. I was just come because it is the practice in Lesotho. I had to go right back to the mountains. But I take only one month in the mountains and I come back to Roma, to be with my mother and to make my church marriage.

CHAPTER 9

Doctors and Babies

Not long after my church marriage, I found I was pregnant again. Alexis was with me in the Maluti, ploughing and looking after the sheep, cows, and horses, and we were happy together with his family. His father liked to weave baskets, and he made big grass baskets – we call them *lisiu* – for maize, looking for a good harvest. 'M'anthunya was working in the field with Alexis, or fetching wood from the forest for fire. I was still learning the Maluti ways, and sometimes I would go with her; sometimes I would go with other women my age.

I was no more a fool; I wanted this baby, so this time I was careful about it. I was often hungry for meat; I craved it. We had chickens, but they belonged to my mother-in-law. She didn't want to kill them. I ask 'M'anthunya for help about what I should do. She said pregnant women always want meat, but this is useless. We don't need it. So one day Alexis's little brother, about twelve years old, went out and caught field-mice for me. He made a fire, and first he roasted them with the skin on. When they were black, he pulled the skin off and tore the stomach to take out the insides and put the little pieces of meat on the fire again. After it's cooked, you can throw the head away, or you can eat it if you like the taste of the brains.

I was curious. I always saw people in Lesotho eating field-mice, but I didn't know that one day I would eat them myself. So I ate it. I found that it's a nice meat, a little bit like pork. You can eat it with *papa*, if you have ten or twelve of them. If you like, you can boil them in water, then take the skin off, and then fry them; you don't need to use fat because they are very fatty from eating maize and wheat. So they have plenty of their own fat, for frying. I ate them all the year of that pregnancy, but I never wanted to eat them again.

When I was six months, I went to see the doctor in Roma because I was not feeling all right. The doctor says again I should be in hospital, but this time I make sure when he means I should go. He says to go when the pains begin; and he says I should go to the clinic every month for a check-up. There is no clinic in the Maluti, but I didn't say anything about that. The doctor gave me medicine to drink and pills. I drank them, but I was still not all right. 'M'anthunya gave me some Basotho medicine, and it made me better.

When I am eight months, I go to Roma, to stay at my mother's house and to wait for the pains to come. When my pains come, I will go to hospital. Right on time, at nine months, the pains come and I go to hospital. The child arrives at night, a baby boy. In the morning my sister-in-law, Sephefu's wife, who was living with my mother, comes to the hospital to see us. He was a healthy baby, and I was healthy. Nothing wrong, nothing bad; I am so happy. But that night after dark the child started to cry, cry, cry. The doctor came and looked at him, but he didn't say anything. Not even a word. He gave the baby water to drink, but the baby cried until his voice was gone. In the morning, about 7 o'clock, the child passed away. When my sister-in-law and mother come to see me, they don't find the child in the bed with me. They say, 'Where is the child?' and pull the blankets aside and search. No child. I cannot speak, because I am crying and my throat is tight. They ask the woman in the bed next to me, 'Where is the child of this woman?'

She says, 'We don't know. He cried the whole night. In the morning he passed away. It's a pity.'

This time I waited a long time for him and tried to do everything right. I was looking at all the other women in the hospital beds with their babies, and me lying there alone. My child dead, again.

My mother and sister-in-law go away and tell Alexis and the family. They have to ride a horse to reach them, to tell them the child was here but it passed away. Alexis's father came to find us, but they told him they buried the baby at the hospital. We never even took him home.

After ten days I go home to my mother's house for a few days and then back to the Maluti, put on a white *tubu* again, and put aside all my good dresses. I choose one dress to wear, because when you wear a white *tubu* you wear only one dress and one blanket the whole month. You wear that dress every day and after the sun has set, you wash and hang it outside to dry in the dark. In the morning you put it on again. So I did all of this, and after that month I was staying at home in the Maluti with Alexis again, wondering why I cannot have a baby like other women.

Alexis decided we should go back to Gauteng so that he can find out what is taking place with these children. Maybe there are no good doctors in Lesotho. So as soon as I am pregnant again, Alexis goes to Benoni. After three months there, he sends me money to come to be with him. I find him in Benoni, working in the gardens of the white people and making blankets in a factory.

When I arrive there he first takes me to a Chinese doctor. The Chinese doctor gives me some medicine to drink, but he doesn't tell us about the children. He just asks how I got the babies, and I tell him. He says, 'You are going to get a baby. Don't worry.'

I say, 'Yes, I can get a baby, but I wonder why the babies die after one or two days.'

He says, 'I wonder.'

So he gave me medicines and pills. I drink them, I drink them. And I wonder. I am going to the clinic there. But then Alexis says we must go to a traditional doctor, a Mosotho born in Gauteng and what we call a 'Zionist' doctor. People call him 'Mosione', or 'Ziona'.

It was in the morning, about nine o'clock, when we arrive. Ziona takes pure water in a basin, and he says, 'Give me ten cents. Put it in the water in this basin.'

Alexis puts it in the water. And Ziona says, 'I am going to tell you a story now. How many were you when you entered this house?'

Alexis says, 'We are only two, me and my wife.'

'No,' the traditional doctor says, 'you are three.'

Alexis and I look at each other. We don't know what this can mean. Then Ziona says, 'You came in, Alexis, and after you there is an old lady with very big breasts. She is taking your wife by the hand, until you sit down. Now she speaks. She says, "I must tell you, Alexis and wife, I am very, very angry, because you don't see what is happening. I am taking these children which are dying, because you don't do what I say you must do."'

We wonder now. We wonder.

Ziona says, 'You are four months pregnant now. Did I ask you how many months are you?'

We say No.

He says, 'You are four months. The old lady wants to kill this wife of yours because she is tired of this.'

Alexis asks, 'Who is the old lady?'

Ziona says, 'Is the grandmother of your wife. The mother of her mother.' He goes on talking, 'When Mpho was born, her mother didn't make a feast, and the old lady is angry for that. So you must go home, Mpho, to your mother's house, and tell your mother that she must take a goat, slit its neck, and remove the gall bladder. Your mother must put the gall bladder in a basin of water and wash you with her hands and this water from head to toes. And after that, the meat of the goat can be eaten by everybody.'

But we were worried from there, because we were far from my mother's home. The Zionist doctor said I must not go back to Alexis's house; I must go straight to my mother's house and do this. It was Sunday, and we could not find the money for the ticket. We must wait till Friday to get the money; then we go to the station where I will leave for Lesotho.

We know the train leaves at half past eight for Germiston, so we arrive at the station at seven. But there is a white man, a Boer, selling the tickets, and he says to us, 'Go away. You are late. You won't find the train.' And he is laughing. We know it is still time, and we are very worried, for I am so late already from the Sunday before. But the man says, 'No. No. Go away!'

Plate One

'There was a heavy snow that year, snow up to my hips if I walked outside. There was so much snow it was blue. When you lift your foot out of the snow, the hollow place looks blue. It was that cold. It was the same snow that brought the cold into Alexis's bones.'

Photograph: *The Natal Witness*

Plate Two

'In Benoni Location
we were living in a nice
concrete-block house
with a corrugated zinc
roof. There were many
houses so close together
you could hear people
talking on every side.'

Photographs
Left and opp: Museum of
Africa, Johannesburg;
Below: Anglo-American
Corporation

'Finally we find the house, a large rondavel and many people, Alexis's family. I like the sounds, the birds and the crickets, the silence. Most of all I like the silence. No fighting, no yelling. It was going to be good life for me.'

Photographs: Victor Glasstone

'At one time Alexis had a very beautiful horse. People believed Alexis was a chief because he was so tall and powerful on his horse. All the other women wanted him.'

Photograph: Anglo-American Corporation

Photographs opposite
Top left: *'M'e* Mpho and her *motsoalle*. *Top right*: *'M'e* Mpho with her children; in the back row are (*L to R*), Manraile, Ralibuseng, Motlatsi; in front are Mofihli and Muso. *Below*: Catholic mission at Marakabei, January 1963. Photograph by David Goldblatt.

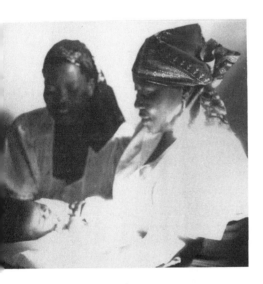

'Nelson Mandela is President of the Republic. I never thought I would see this in my life, and I am happy to live at this time. Now we can all have new dreams. We can build something new.'

Clockwise: *'M'e* Mpho with the current *'M'*anthunya and her baby; in Durban; with one of her grandsons, Tumisang Kuoe; and with Limakatso Kendall.

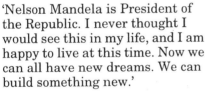

Other people come and take tickets for Germiston while we are waiting, and Alexis tries again. But the Boer shouts at us, 'No! What are you waiting for? Go home. Come back tomorrow.'

We were sad and heavy, because we have prepared everything for going. We go back to the Location. When we arrive there, we have to go back to the Zionist doctor and tell him what has happened and ask him what is going on.

Ziona says, 'Yes, it should be like that. The old lady is angry; she makes the way difficult. You waste time. But kneel down. I'll pray for you to go to work on this problem and find a solution. Kneel down. Let me pray.'

And we kneel, and he prays, asking God for a good journey to help us go well. Then we go back to our house. There we meet my brother, Sephefu, who was working in Benoni. He comes to give me five pounds (we called it five pounds then, it was about ten rands) to give to my mother.

At seven o'clock the next day we go to the station. There we see the same Boer selling tickets. He sells us the ticket without any complaint and laughs at us. I go then alone to Germiston, where I am going to find the train for Lesotho. From there I go to Bloemfontein, then straight to Maseru. At that time white people took the first-class car and black people the second-class car. Also in the station there is one part for whites, another for blacks. There was no food on the train, but in the morning a person comes selling tea and fills our flasks if we can pay.

When I arrived in Maseru I took a bus straight to Roma, and there I go on foot to my mother's house in Mafikeng. It was in the same place as my house is now, a little rondavel. And when I saw my mother I told her everything the Zionist doctor said to us. Then my mother heard me and cried and cried, and said, 'My mother knows that I am poor. Where will I get the goat? She knows I have nothing to buy a goat with, and I don't know where to buy one.' So we slept. When I was still sleeping in the morning, my mother takes her rosary and says, 'I am going; I will tell you when I get back.'

I didn't know where she was going. She went to a person who had goats and sheep, and she was praying her rosary, 'God help me to find a goat.'

When she arrived there she told the man, '*Ntate*, Mpho arrived yesterday. She says my mother says I must have a goat for making the feast which I could not do when Mpho was born. But I don't know where to find such a goat.'

The man answered, 'Oh *Ausi*, I have some goats and sheep, and these goats and sheep are for those things. Give me four pounds.'

She says, 'I am going to talk with Mpho at home to tell her that I found the goat, so don't give it to anybody else. I will come back with the money.'

And then she comes home to me, and I tell her my brother gave me the money for this purpose in Benoni, so I give it to her.

So come the goat with the shepherd, and we slaughter, and I am washed: my head, face, everything, with warm water and the goat's gall bladder. And after finishing that, the next day I have to prepare to go back to Benoni. I take a little bit of meat to go and give to Alexis when I get home.

Alexis ate the bit of goat, and I told him all that had been done. He was very glad and prayed God, if God can hear our prayer, to ask the old lady to be comforted. I was going to the clinic every month, and when the time came, on the 25th of July 1952, I got a nine-pound baby boy. The nurses were good to me and the doctors were flying all around me, because they want to see what happened. Here was a woman who had two babies, and one died after one day; the other after a day and a half. Now this third one was very healthy, and I had a good birth: no scissors, no cutting, no nothing. It hurt coming out, because it was so big, but I was very happy. We named the child Tseliso, which means 'Consolation', and he grew strong and big very quickly. I thought that our troubles with these babies were over, but I was wrong.

I was in the hospital for ten days, and then I went home to our house in Benoni. We didn't have any family around to help me, so Alexis was helping me to do everything, watching Tseliso grow very quickly. We were glad to see that this child is going to live, and after three months I came home to Lesotho from Gauteng to show the people my child.

First I went to see my mother, in Roma. I take only two days there and go again to the mountains. I had to walk that long way alone, because there were no brothers, no sisters who could go with me. Just me and the baby, walking by foot. When I got half the way, in Makhaleng, I found a lady who could walk with me to Marakabei, and she carried the baby with me.

When we arrive at home, everybody is very glad to see us. 'M'anthunya takes the baby and kisses it. Everybody is crying and laughing and singing, and *Ntate* tells the boys to find a sheep. So they showed Tseliso the sheep. They say, 'This is your sheep,' so he can know it is his feast, and then they slaughter the sheep and we eat the meat with all the family and many friends who come. I stay there while I am nursing Tseliso, until he is ten months old. Then I must wean Tseliso, because we say if a child comes after two babies who have died, he must not nurse more than ten months. So I wean Tseliso, and I go back to Alexis, in Benoni.

In Benoni we have a whole house of our own, a government house. It was early 1950s, and the government of Gauteng gave us houses at that time. I take only three months after I am back with Alexis, and I am pregnant again. In June 1954, I've got a baby boy. This one is big again – eight pounds, fifteen ounces – and he is healthy and I am healthy too. It begins to look like Alexis and I are going to be all right together in Gauteng. But my heart was not happy there, because I loved the mountains, and I missed them. I went back to Lesotho alone, leaving Alexis because he had to stay where he had work.

But June – his real name was Mikaele, but we call him June because he was born in June – he take only two years and he was dead. First he began to be painful in the stomach. The time when he is crying, when I put my hand on his stomach I can feel something going up and down. He started to cry all the time, cry and cry. He can't eat or sleep. I take him to the doctor in Roma, and the doctor can't do anything. He says he doesn't see anything wrong, gives him medicine. Medicine does no good. It takes only a few days and he passed.

This was very hard for me, because I loved this child like Tseliso, and I thought the bad times of the babies dying was over. June was a beautiful boy, a sweet boy, laughing and singing to himself on my back while I was working, and I let myself love him too much. I thought June was growing up like Tseliso. After the burial at Roma I have to go to the Maluti again and wear a *tubu* again, but not a white *tubu* this time. It was 1956, and I was twenty-six years old. I have lost three babies and kept one. I feel sorry for myself at that time, but I know it is good that I have kept the one baby.

It's very horrible for a woman in Lesotho if she have no baby, because then she must always be alone with her husband, feeling something wrong, asking God why this is happening to her. People will laugh at her and say bad things about her. They will tell her husband, 'Your wife doesn't want to make children. You have to beat her.'

She can think it's the man's fault she have no baby, but she can't go to another man to make a baby with her. Others will tell her husband, and he can kill her, or beat her until she wants to die.

There is nobody who doesn't want a baby. What will a woman do if she have no baby? Just work and work, take care of a man, get beatings when he drinks *joala*. There is nothing to make her laugh, nothing to take her mind off her troubles, no small hand holding hers, no child singing on her back to make the work lighter.

I have a friend in the Maluti named Julia. She loved me and loved my children, but she have no baby. Even until this day, she have no baby. When Tseliso was small, and Julia sees me, she always asks how am I, says how beautiful is my child. When we are alone she asks me to tell her what she must do, so she can have a baby. She tells me that many times she gets pregnant, but when it's two months or three months it goes out, and she is always sick. She asks me why. I wonder what I can do. She goes to every kind of doctor – Basotho doctors, English doctors – no baby. Even now her man is always hitting her, saying, 'You never wanted to have a baby!' He points to other women, says, 'That lady has a baby.'

She will cry.

Then he says, 'Don't talk to me. Why don't you have a baby?'

So she always cries, cries to me and says, 'I don't know what I can do. Please tell your mother I want a baby and ask her to pray for me.' Everyone knows my mother is very good at praying.

So my mother prayed for Julia to have a baby, but it refused. One night my mother was praying, and the words came to her, 'Here is a baby boy, but I don't know what you will do with him.' This prayer worried my mother, and she wondered about these words until she passed away, but Julia never got a baby.

The last time my daughter-in-law went to the Maluti, she heard that Julia is still living out in the mountains, a day's walk from Marakabei. She must be my age, now, sixty or so. Her husband is still alive and treating her very badly. They say she is very thin and poor, and she has no one to talk to but this husband, who hates her. Even if she is sick, her husband says, 'Wake up and prepare food for me, you woman who will not have a baby.'

I will not see her again. I just write letters, and when my daughter-in-law, 'M'athuso, goes to see her family in Marakabei, I send soap or sugar. This is why I say there is nobody who doesn't want a baby. Nobody wants this life.

CHAPTER 10

The Sugar Crisis

In 1957 I got another baby, a tiny girl. She was so small we didn't know if she could live, but we called her Manraile, which means a very small thing. Then Alexis and I decided it is time for us to stay in the Maluti and raise these children, and no more living in Benoni. Tseliso was now five years old, and we think it is better for him to be in the mountains than in Benoni, where there is too much noise and fighting. Since 1955 Alexis had no work in Benoni anyway, so why should we stay? This was the beginning of my best time of life until now, but Alexis was always threatening to take me away.

Tseliso learned to look after the small lambs and calves. I was working in the field and in the house, with little Manraile on my back. Alexis was working in the fields. At that time I learned how to make maize meal with a grinding stone; I learned where to find wood in the forest. I was knowing everything about how to live in the Maluti. The men plant. The women harvest. The old men make grass baskets and thatch for the roofs of rondavels, and they sell them in the valleys. The women cook and do hand-sewing. Some women have hand-operated sewing machines. All day you are watching the babies play, and they make you laugh. Or you look up and you see the mountains, the clouds passing over them. You hear the wide open quiet, and you feel that God is close to you. In the evening when the work is done, the people talk, sing, tell stories. No radios, no cars or buses. For somebody now, it would seem very boring, but to us it was a way of life which was good.

My heart always liked to be in the mountains, but Alexis worried about me, because when I was living in the mountains I came to be very thin and dark. One day Alexis said, 'You are foolish, 'M'atsepo, because when you are in Roma, in only a few days you are fat; but here, I tell them to kill the sheep so you can eat it with *papa*, but you are still thin. In Roma you stay with an old lady who has nothing to eat; people take pity on her and give her a little bit of maize. But you are fat when you are there. Why? It looks like I don't love you, I don't feed you in the mountains. People will say you are not sitting nicely with my family in the Maluti.'

I laugh to Alexis, and I say, 'I like the Maluti. I am happy here. Maybe the Maluti don't like me, I don't know. But I don't mind what people say because I am thin.'

He says, 'I have decided we are going to stay in Roma, both of us. I want to have a fat wife. Maybe I can find work in Roma.'

I say No. I tell him Roma is a town, and I don't want to be in a town. I tell him, 'Roma reminds me of Benoni. I was staying in Benoni too long. I don't like towns. My heart doesn't want to be there. I like to be a Mosotho in the Maluti.' I tell him I like the mountains, the sky, the space, no crowding. I tell him we can live together nicely in the Maluti, even if we have no money. And we don't know if he can find work in Roma, so maybe if we come to Roma we can be even worse, because we won't have the fields for maize. But Alexis was not happy. He went on thinking.

I take two years and I was pregnant again. I got a baby boy, Motlatsi, born April 5 1959. We named him Motlatsi because it means 'the boy who comes to help'. We said he came to help Tseliso, because June passed away. I came down to Roma to have the child, and after ten days in hospital, I went to my mother's house in Mafikeng to stay until the baby was three months. And I got fat, so fat, the way I always did when I stayed with my mother.

Alexis arrived to see the child. As soon as my mother was out of the room, he said, 'Look how fat are you! But at home you don't want to be fat like this. Look at this poor old lady, your mother. She has gone out to pick *moroho* for you. I bring you meat of a sheep to eat with *papa*, but you say you want only *moroho* with your *papa*. How can you be so fat and you eat only *papa* and *moroho*? Really this is not good.'

I answer him, 'Oh, don't mind. Maybe in Roma the water likes me, and the climate likes me. In the Maluti I'm going to be dark and thin, but so what. My heart likes the Maluti. You must let me stay there.'

When Motlatsi is three months, Alexis goes with me back to the Maluti, in wintertime. We go to the field for harvesting maize and sorghum, and again we are hoeing the ground. I came to be thin again, and it was snowing and there was ice on the fields.

To stay warm we have a fire inside the house every morning and even all day, until we go to sleep. When you wake up it is so cold that the water in the bucket has frozen. If there was any water on the floor, it is ice. We sleep with sheepskins on top of our blankets, and we are warm under them, but it's hard to get out of bed in the morning into that cold.

Between 1955 and 1959 we were very poor because in all those years Alexis had no work, but in 1959 Alexis found work building roads in the mountains and working on a dam, and everything was better. It is good we can't see the future, because I didn't know this job was going to kill Alexis. I was just happy with the children, making our life in the fields and watching our sheep grow until we were some of the richest farmers in Marakabei. We had over two hundred sheep, ten goats, thirty cattle, five horses, and some donkeys.

We used the money Alexis made on the roads to buy things we needed from the shop. There was just one shop in Marakabei; it was a half-day walk to the shop from our home, and a half-day back. We would take the donkeys with sacks of maize for grinding in the machine, and we could bring back paraffin for the lamp, soap for washing, maybe some candles, tea, and sugar. It was that sugar that led to the crisis between my mother-in-law and me.

I was always liking sugar, even when I was a girl still living at home. My mother and father liked sugar, because they were not drinking *joala*. We say sugar is our *joala*. But my mother-in-law was always grumbling about the sugar. She called me Moroa because I liked sugar so much. (Baroa is our name for the San people. The South Africans call them 'Bushmen'.) I was not using much sugar – just a little in my tea, if I have tea. But 'M'anthunya said, 'Alexis leaves this girl here and she eats the sugar like the Baroa. She always wants to eat sugar. Can't live without sugar.'

'M'anthunya and I were always staying together nicely until this time. She had nothing. I had nothing. We would grind dried peas and roast them to make a kind of coffee because we had no tea, and she would drink this thing without sugar. I didn't like it; it tasted nasty to me. I don't like anything made with dried peas. I just waited all those years, hoping some day we can have proper tea with sugar again. But when Alexis began making money, and we had the chance to buy sugar, it looked like 'M'anthunya was jealous of the money we spent on sugar. She was always grumbling.

One day Alexis comes home from work with sugar and tea, and he says, 'You must take care of this sugar, because you like it.'

Some days later, Alexis asked for tea with sugar. I look for the sugar. No sugar.

He says, 'Why is there no sugar? I bought sugar.'

I say, 'I don't know.'

He asks his mother, 'Where is the sugar?'

She says, 'I don't know. I'm not a Moroa. I don't know anything about sugar. I don't use it. My children don't use it.'

Alexis asked her, 'From when?' Because he knew she would use sugar every chance she got. So he asked his two sisters, 'Where is the sugar?'

They say they don't know.

Then 'M'anthunya becomes angry. She grumbles more, and finally she shouts at him, 'You must take your wife and live away from my house, because you accuse my children of eating your sugar.'

We had a new rondavel on a hill nearby, but it was just a storage room with no fire. Alexis said, 'When I go to work, you should move to that new rondavel. Take everything and go there.'

So next day when I wake up, Alexis goes to work and I take all my things and my three-legged pot which my mother bought me, and I move to that rondavel. I take the things which belonged to my mother-in-law in that rondavel and put them in another storage place by her house. And I go to the field to pick *moroho*.

'M'anthunya asks one of Alexis's sisters who was only ten years old, 'What is your sister doing?'

'I don't know.'

'Why doesn't she tell me she is moving to that house? What makes her so angry, that she takes her things and goes there?'

The little girl says, 'We don't know. Maybe it's the sugar.'

'Oh!' 'M'anthunya says. 'Then she can stay there alone, I don't care. I won't even give her a child to help her.'

In Lesotho if a daughter-in-law goes to a house apart from the mother-in-law, the older woman gives her a child to help her with the work. So when 'M'anthunya said this, it was because she was very angry with me.

I stayed in the rondavel. I slept. 'M'anthunya never asked anything. When I woke up she didn't say anything to me, just looked at me and I looked at her. It was a kind of silent war. Tseliso was going up and down. Sometimes he would eat with me; sometimes with his grandmother.

So at the end of the month Alexis came home again. When he arrived at home, he greeted his mother and father. He arrived just before sunset. He sat with them, talking. When the sun had set, he asked, 'Where is 'M'atsepo?'

They say, 'She has gone out to that rondavel. We think she is angry. We don't know why. Maybe it's your fault.' They were afraid to tell him. But the rondavel where I was staying was not a great distance away, maybe fifty metres. So he picked up his bag and came up to the rondavel where I was. He greeted me, laughing, and said, 'Yes, you see. I have told you to do this, and it is time you did it. You have all that you need now. I have been a long time telling you that you must be out of that house. You stayed there six years, and finally you see that you are enough by yourself. This is good. You don't need my mother for anything.'

'Yes,' I said. 'I see that I am enough by myself.' And we were happy together that night in our house alone.

So Alexis takes only two days with me, and he must go back to work. As he is leaving he tells me, 'My mother told me to bring back sugar the next time I come home.' And we laughed. But from that time I never lived in his parents' house again.

CHAPTER 11

Khotso, Pula, Nala

Lesotho has a motto: *Khotso, Pula, Nala*. It means Peace, Rain, Prosperity. We say these words as if they are prayers for what we don't have. But in the best days of my life at Marakabei, all three came to me for a time, and I was living in grace. I'd got many sheep – two hundred of them, ten goats, thirty cattle, and five horses. I don't want goats; they are too stupid, so I had only ten or twenty goats. Tseliso was looking after these animals with some other boys – Tseliso, his brother Motlatsi, and two boys who stayed with me, Pakiso and Sello. But sometimes when the boys were not there, maybe going to the shops to find maize meal, I used to go with the sheep in the mountains. I would go with Manraile on my back when she was still small, before the rest of my boys were born.

I was very glad at that time. I could look all around me at the animals, at the fields, and it's mine. All these sheep are mine. I go early in the morning, maybe about 8 a.m., and start back at 4 p.m. because we had to go a long way in the mountains. I'm going up and down, up and down, not sitting down the whole day, because the sheep would run away if I could sit down. When I arrive at home, around 6 p.m., I would be very tired. But it was no use, because I have to cook for the boys who have gone to Marakabei to buy *phofo*.

It was work, but it was fine to me at that time, because I was not short of anything. My husband was still alive, and he had work, so we had some money to buy things. I had a big rondavel and a square *huisie*, and another small rondavel for a kitchen, we called it a *mokhoro*, a hut. It's where we cooked and where the shepherds slept. When I was out all day, I might take a tin of *motoho* to drink, a little slice of bread, and nothing else. It was all I wanted.

Manraile was not hungry because I was still nursing her. If I had no milk in my breast, I would catch a goat and milk it into the mouth of Manraile. She liked it. I like it better when it's cooked, because I don't like the smell of the wild sage in the goat's milk.

I was also collecting firewood in the mountains, we call it *patsi*. Sometimes I collect wild vegetables, *moroho*, too. (I don't collect wild mushrooms – only the shepherds eat them. Some women who look after sheep also eat mushrooms like the boys, but I never ate them, except in soup.) When I'm out in the mountain meadows, my mind is watching the sheep all the time, because sometimes I can lose some of them under the rocks. Even though I have two hundred, I count them again and again to be sure I don't lose them. I was thanking God to have so many sheep, because when I was in Gauteng I used to say, 'If I can get sheep, it will be OK to me.' When I was in Benoni, living in the mountains and having sheep was only a dream. But even before I lived in the Maluti I felt it would be good to be there. Maybe every Mosotho feels this, wherever they live.

So when I arrive at Alexis's home we buy ten sheep, and they make such a lot. We were eating meat every month. Even so our flock grows from ten to two hundred, because every year in September or October the sheep get babies, and the goats get their babies in July.

When I go home from the *naheng* I cook *papa* and *moroho*, sometimes with meat. The boys or the men kill the sheep, and we have meat. Sometimes I cook *bohobe*, steamed bread, for taking to the fields or the mountains with the sheep.

In the evening we sit and tell stories. Children ask for stories of the old days, like I tell them about my life when I was in Gauteng, and stories of their father when he took me to the Maluti. I tell them I was afraid of the horse, but one day when I was tired, I learned to ride the horse. When the horse is going up the hills I learn to lean backwards, not to fall off on my head. The children laugh at me. They think I was a fool when I was young, and it's true.

When Alexis was at home we were staying together *hantle*. We loved one another. It was not easy, but if your husband loves you, it's good. Everybody in the village used to say, 'This Alexis and wife always sit together nicely. Did they ever shout at one another?'

They used to talk so when they passed our house on the way to fetch water. They talk about our house. They tell me I am always good to my husband, and my husband is very good to me, and all that they say is true.

When people make feasts, like for marriage or for a funeral, we go together. When we arrive, Alexis stops with the men, and I stay with the women, but we are still together there. We had a good marriage, even better than my mother and father, and I know that this does not happen for many people.

At one time Alexis had a very beautiful horse, and the King saw it. The King asked him what he fed the horse.

Alexis told him, oats.

The King asked where to find these oats. And Alexis told the King how to find the best oats in the mountains. From that day, he was friends with the King. He would sometimes go to Matsieng, where the King lived, and supervise the men who were growing oats for the King. When he arrived there, he would tell the gate-keeper, 'I want to talk to Bereng,' who was the King.

The gate-keeper would say, 'Who are you? Tell us what you want to say, and we will take the message.'

He would say, 'Go and tell him Morena Moalosi Nthunya is here.'

When they told the King, the King would say, 'Bring him to me!'

And the people would say, 'Who is this man?' But they believed Alexis was a chief, because he was so tall and powerful on his horse. All the other women wanted him. They would sometimes say, 'Alexis, why don't you love me? I love you.'

Then he would come home and tell me what they said, and we would laugh. I would say, 'OK, why don't you love them?'

He would say, 'They are mad. They don't know I will come and tell you what they say.'

I was never afraid he would leave me for one of these women. I think it was because I trusted myself; I knew I would never leave him. So I thought he would never leave me. When he wanted another woman, he could have her. He would come and tell me, 'I love this woman. Can you tell her?'

I would say, 'No. I don't want to tell her.'

Then he would say, 'I wanted you to know first.'

I might say, 'Her man will hit you.'

Alexis would laugh at this. He was not afraid. We were the same. When I would fall in love with another man, I could have men-friends, the same that Alexis could have women-friends. He didn't mind about my friends, and I didn't mind about his. He knew, but he didn't want my men-friends to know that he knew. We were just playing; it was not serious, and we both knew that it would never be serious. I would never have a man-friend unless his wife loved me too, and didn't mind. If there was a woman who didn't want me to love her husband, I wouldn't do it. Life was different in that time.

If I was in love with another man for a while, Alexis could be friends with him. We might ask him to our house and make a feast; it was no trouble. Even the postman, the one who gave me a ride to Marakabei when I was going for the first time, one day Alexis came to me and said, ''M'atsepo, come and greet your husband. This man gave you a ride up into the Maluti, and you would never have come here without his help.'

So I greeted him, and kissed him, but we were not in love. When the people saw this, they said, 'Does Alexis love this wife of his?'

Others say, 'Yes! He loves her very much, but he knows she is his wife, and she will be his wife until one of them dies.' It was true.

Even our mothers, they used to tell us that they could be in love with other men, they could share the blankets with them, but their husbands would not make a clash or a fight with that man. Most people were not jealous like they are now; some were, but most were at peace with each other. If you are jealous, it is because you don't trust yourself. Then you are not really loving the other person; you want to own them, like you own a cow.

Now people are not at peace as we always used to be. Now if a woman falls in love with a man who is not her husband, and her husband finds out about it, they are going to fight. One may even kill the other one. I don't know why these things have changed. I wonder about it, but I don't understand.

Alexis said he always wanted me to greet every man who greets me. If I want to kiss him, I should kiss him. Alexis was trusting me; I was trusting him. Alexis would sometimes drink too much; he was a drinker. But when he was drinking, he was never angry with me.

When we came to be rich, our neighbours got jealous; even the parents of Alexis were jealous. *Ntate* Nthunya tried many times to take our lambs. He said they were his, and Alexis and his father would fight.

One time *Ntate* Nthunya told Alexis's younger brothers and sisters that Alexis took his sheep. So then those children turned against Alexis, and there was trouble in the family. They were always fighting with Alexis. When *Ntate* isn't fighting, Alexis will start. This was a trouble to me, because I never saw people fighting when I was growing up. We left Benoni to get away from the fighting, and when we were poor in the Maluti, there was peace there. But when we came to be rich, there was no more peace. My heart was heavy, and I started to worry. When Alexis came from the fields, he would pass the place where they sold *joala*, and by the time he passed his mother's house he would be drunk and angry, ready for a fight. Many times he would walk into his mother's house and say, 'Give me food!'

His own sisters would answer, 'No! Go to your own house and eat. Your wife can cook for you.'

Then he would hit the girls, and they would fight back, yelling and shouting. Then 'M'anthunya would cry, 'Oh, 'M'atsepo, help! Help! Alexis is hitting us.'

So I would come, and when I arrived I would just say, 'Let's go home, Alexis. Why are you fighting here?'

He would smile at me and say, 'I will kill them one day.' Then he would say to his mother, 'If it was not for this good wife I married, I was going to kill you.'

Then his mother would say, 'She has given you a medicine to make you love her so much. You don't love us any more. You love the mother of your wife more than you love me.'

Alexis would say, 'Yes, I love the mother of 'M'atsepo because she respects me. You don't respect me, and you teach your children not to respect me.'

This same fight happened many times, and it was always the same words we were saying to each other. In our own house, Alexis and I always slept in peace. Sometimes I would ask him, 'Why do you always fight with your parents? They begin to think it is my fault.'

He says, 'Everybody in this village knows it's not you. My mother is not nice to me. My father tries to steal my lambs. My sisters take my father's side. We all know where the trouble is, and we know it is not with you. So go to sleep, my wife, and let me take care of my troublesome family.'

We stayed like that until 'M'anthunya died, and Alexis was drinking much *joala* all those years. After 'M'anthunya passed away and I became the head of the family, I was able to keep peace in the family most of the time. But Alexis kept drinking *joala*, and he was very fierce, we call it *bohale*. When he was no more fighting with his family, he would fight with other people. Sometimes our neighbours would come to me to borrow *phofo*, if Alexis was not at home, but they were afraid to come when he was there. Everyone stayed far away from us when Alexis was drinking.

CHAPTER 12

When a Woman Loves a Woman

When I was living in the mountains I got a special friend. She was living in another village, and I passed her house when I was going to church every month. One day she saw me and said, 'What is your name?'

I told her I was 'M'atsepo Nthunya. So she said, 'I always see you passing here. Today I want to talk to you. I want you to be my *motsoalle*.' This is a name we have in Sesotho for a very special friend. She says, 'I love you.'

It's like when a man chooses you for a wife, except when a man chooses, it's because he wants to share the blankets with you. The woman chooses you the same way, but she doesn't want to share the blankets. She wants love only. When a woman loves another woman, you see, she can love her with a whole heart.

I saw how she was looking at me, and I said, '*Ke hantle*, it's fine with me.' So she kissed me, and from that day she was my *motsoalle*. She told her husband about it, and he came to my house and told my husband, and these two husbands became friends too. It was a long distance from my house to her house, and she was lonely because she had no children. It was only her and her husband.

Most of the time I would only see her once a month, when I went to church. We would meet outside her house and walk to church together. She would sit by me in church, and we would hold hands. There was a café near her village, and when I went to the café, I would meet her, or if she was not around I would see a child and say, 'Go tell 'M'e 'M'alineo I'm here in the café.' Then she would come, and we would talk until it's time for me to go.

She loved me so much that she bought me a *seshoeshoe* dress and two brooms. One day my *motsoalle* said she wanted me to come her house for a feast to celebrate our friendship. She cooked for days to get ready, and even me, I made much bread and *joala* and two chickens to add to her feast. I went to her house with five women, my husband, and two other men.

When we arrive at her house we find that she has prepared a sheep. She shows us the sheep and says, 'There is your food.' It was like a wedding.

So we say our thanks, and they take the sheep and slaughter it. We go into the house and begin singing, everyone feeling happy. We sing while we wait for the meat, and those who drink *joala*, drink all day. Those who don't drink *joala* have *motoho* and Coke. So when the food is ready and the meat is cooked, then we sit down. We eat meat, bread, samp, everything we can think of. It was summer, so it was hot. We stayed the whole day. In the afternoon, around six, I kissed my *motsoalle* goodbye and we went back to our village, singing all the way. I remember it was late, about ten, when we got home, walking by foot, and when we got home we kept on singing till two o'clock in the morning.

As soon as light came, our neighbours came and began drinking what was left of the *joala*. There was much left. The only ones who don't drink are me and another lady. I never liked *joala*. My mother and father both never drank *joala*, even my brother Sephefu, we didn't like it. But we didn't mind if other people wanted it. Still, we were tired from all that walking and singing and drinking and eating meat all day.

Another time, a year later, my *motsoalle* comes for a feast at my house. So she comes with many women and many husbands carrying *joala* and *motoho*. They arrive at noon or so, and we took the whole day. When they arrived I showed them the sheep, and after that we slaughtered it and cooked it. There were many people coming for the party. All these people knew that my *motsoalle* was visiting and they came to honour us for loving each other. We bring some of the people inside the house, and the rest of the people who came for the feast stayed outside. Those inside were singing, waiting for their food. Those outside were dancing. So when we finished cooking, we put all the food on big dishes – meat in one dish, bread in another, and many drums of *joala*. I call my *motsoalle* and say, 'There is your food.'

So I stand up and feed the people inside and outside. They were dancing all day. I had a wind-up gramophone with two loudspeakers, and I put on the music – jive records, African jive. I got the records in Maseru.

I gave her a dress Alexis bought in Maseru and a *doek* to match. They stayed the whole day until it was about seven, but they had to go then. They were a little drunk, and they had a long way to walk. They took *joala* in five-litre buckets to drink on the way home. So in the morning there were still some people drinking outside and inside, jiving and dancing and having a good time.

Alexis says to them, 'Oh, you must go to your houses now. The *joala* is finished.'

They say, 'We want meat.'

He gives them the empty pot to show them the meat is all gone. But the ladies who are drinking don't care. They say, 'We are not here to see you; we are coming to see 'M'atsepo.'

They sleep, they sing, they dance. Some of them are *motsoalle* together with each other. I go out to talk with them, but they are too drunk to understand. They tell me, 'We are jiving here, just wind up that gramophone so we can dance.'

I say, 'I'm tired. I need to sleep,' but I am laughing, because I am happy; it is all feeling so nice.

After that, my *motsoalle* sometimes sends me green maize or peas if I have none. We always sit together at church. We stay very good friends. But after some years, my *motsoalle* left her husband to find work in Maseru. He was not treating her well, and they had no children, so it was hard for her to stay alone with him in the mountains.

In Maseru she could not find work. She became a drunkard. I was very sad for that. I saw her last year, on the street. She is no longer my *motsoalle* because she's drinking too much. She was ashamed when she looked at me. I met her selling *moroho* outside a store. I greeted her. I asked her, 'What's the matter with your face?' It was swollen, and she looked very old.

She said, 'It's because I'm poor. I'm working very hard. My husband doesn't want me any more. Sometimes I have nothing to eat.'

I said, 'But you left your husband first.'

She said, 'Yes, because the man was not sleeping at home, so I left him. But now I am tired and want to go home, and my husband married another wife.' So she is still in Maseru, and her husband is near Maseru with another woman. They have been away from the mountains a long time.

In the old days friendship was very beautiful – men friends and women friends. Friendship was as important as marriage. Now this custom is gone; everything is changing. People now don't love like they did long ago. Today the young girls only want men friends; they don't know how to choose women friends. Maybe these girls just want money. Women never have money, so young girls, who want money more than love, get AIDS from these men at the same time they get the money.

CHAPTER 13

The Small Woman

Manraile grew up fast and hard, because she was my only daughter. When she was just six she started to be my helper in the house. She was always going up and down with me; whenever I would leave Marakabei to come to Roma, maybe to come and see my mother, we always went together, walking by foot with no shoes, two of us, and I always had a baby boy on my back. When I was tired, she took the boy on her back to let me rest.

When she was eight I fell sick for a time, so she had to look after the boys and feed them before they went to the fields. She had to wash the baby and carry it, because I always had a baby on my back, always. She was very small, but she had to grind mealies or wheat. She knew how to fry the grains and grind them and make a wheat porridge, dark brown.

We were me and Manraile, plus my four boys and the two other boys who were staying with us. She would work till she slept, and in the morning she would wake up and do it all again. Another day she must cook *lihobe*, it's wheat with peas, you cook it in a big pot. When the boys arrived from *naheng* they must come and eat, and drink milk because we had many cows. They could drink sour milk or fresh milk, they could choose what they wanted. And they slept without hunger.

When Alexis started to be sick, we started to be poor. No food in the house. I used to go in the field with Manraile in the morning to pick green peas in a sack, maybe twenty-five kg. When we arrive at home, after picking all the morning, we sit down and shell them. After finishing that we go to the forest to find some wood and come back again, and cook these peas. No *papa*, no porridge, only these peas. We eat these peas and drink milk, but we get tired of them. So one day a lady asks me, 'Why do you always go to the field every day to find peas? You don't want dried peas?'

I say, 'I like dried peas, but I don't have any. I am just doing what I can do, because my children have nothing to eat.'

'Why didn't you tell us? We didn't know that you had no *phofo*, because you were never so poor. Maybe you are poor now because your husband is not here, but we are not used to thinking that you are poor.'

I say, 'It's true, my husband is sick in the hospital.'

So this lady says, 'When you cook these peas, when they are almost finished being cooked, if someone can give you a handful of *phofo*, put it in the pot. This will make the peas thick so your children can eat them and be full.'

One day I try this. I find that it's a nice food, and my children eat and sleep. They say they are not hungry that day. This way I begin to learn what others know, and I see that I was lucky before, when I did not have to know these things.

Manraile was always working beside me, never complaining. She have no chance to play, but she seemed like she didn't mind. Sometimes I felt shame for the child who always works, never plays. Sometimes I say, 'Go and play! I will try to do everything.'

But many times she refused, because she likes to help me. I worried because she had no shoes, but she said, 'When I'm big I will try to go to my uncle in Roma and find shoes, because he works in a store. He can help me.'

When Alexis was working, Manraile used to have a nice blanket to wear, but when the nice blankets were worn out, I had to buy her a cheap one, an ugly gray one of very rough wool. But she said she liked it, she said, *'Ke hantle, 'M'e,'* and she acted like it was a beautiful blanket. She said that to make me feel better, because it was the best I could do for her. She was wearing a nice *thethana* of beads, not string. But she had no shirt. When it's cold she covers herself with a blanket.

There was no school in Marakabei. In those days I didn't care about my children's schooling. I thought we would go on living in Marakabei always, and there the education of books was not important. What was important was the education of how to live in the mountains, how to work, how to find food and cook it.

Manraile had to know how to carry things on her head, where to find water, how to gather firewood and which kinds of wood will burn a long time without so much smoke. She had to know how to smear the floors and the walls of a house with dung and water. Sometimes Manraile would also go to *naheng*; maybe the boys have gone to Marakabei to grind mealies, so she has to go to *naheng* to look after the sheep. She had to learn how to control the animals, too. She must count them; must know how to turn them if they are going in the wrong direction; how to keep them out of people's fields; and how to nurse them if they are hurt.

I taught her that when a girl wakes up she must go to the stream for water, first thing. The second thing, she must sweep inside, and sweep the ground outside the house. I taught her how to cook, she learned from watching me. And then she must know how to grind mealies, so she won't be like me when I came to Marakabei. I said, 'You will be a fool like me if you don't know how to grind mealies.' My education that I got in school in Benoni was useless in Marakabei. All of the languages I spoke – Tswana, Zulu, Pedi, Xhosa, Afrikaans, English – these were useless in Marakabei. At the same time I didn't know Sesotho things. I only started to learn them when I was grown. So I didn't worry about my children getting this useless education with books.

Manraile learned songs and games when she played with other children, we call them *lipina tsa mokopu*, songs of girls playing. The church was too far for us to get to. But on the first of the month we go for Holy Communion at a little school where the priest comes. The rest of the month there is no priest, so we only pray among ourselves. Sometimes after two months a priest comes to the little school to baptise the small children, and people who are too sick to go to Marakabei can go there – it was still a great distance, it takes half a day to walk there and half a day to walk back home. So I have to teach my children about Christian beliefs myself.

When Manraile was eight and we came to Roma and stayed with my mother, my mother taught her all the prayers and told her about God. Then after Alexis died, Manraile started to go to school, to Roma Primary, and she liked it very much. There were many children of all ages, just starting to school, so she didn't feel ashamed. She was smart in school. Sometimes when she brought home her exercise books I would look at them and talk to her about them. I was happy, because she was going to learn how to write a letter to her man-friends, or to anybody who wants to write. There were books at the school, but people did not have books in their houses. They still don't – not the people I know. Children didn't think about reading at home; it was just a thing you did at school.

When we began living in Roma, Manraile's life got a little bit easier. She was still working hard with her grandmother, but it was not so hard as life in Marakabei. In Roma she didn't have to grind mealies with a stone. She just had to sweep, smear the floors and the walls, fetch water, and wash the laundry. Sometimes I'm there, sometimes I'm still in Marakabei. Her grandmother helped her.

She loved her grandmother very much. My mother also loved her, and she used to tell Manraile that she went to Fatima, it's a special shrine at a town called Ha Ramabanta, to ask for me to have a girl. Because I always made boys. So my mother prayed, asking God to give me a girl. And this was the girl. My mother used to say, 'When you have no girl, nobody will look after you when you are sick. So it's better to pray and ask for a girl. God will help you.'

I used to pray, but I could never pray like my mother. I remember one day after my husband passed away, my mother said to me, 'You must pray that God will not give you another child, because Alexis is dead.' If I have a baby after my husband is dead, people will ask me who this child belongs to, and I will be ashamed. My mother knew I was young, and I was going to share the blankets. But since my husband was dead, I could not afford to feed another child. I could not feed the ones I had.

So I said, 'Yes, I will pray.'

She said, 'Oh my God, I'll help you, because I know you don't know anything. You pray, but you pray as you are talking.'

I say, 'Yes, 'M'e, it's better if you help me.'

She started to pray. We go early, six o'clock to Mass for nine days, waking early, going to Mass, asking God not to give me any more children, because these children are enough. And I never was pregnant again, from that time.

When Alexis was alive and I used to be pregnant, I would have certain dreams: if it's a girl I'll dream I'm being chased by snakes; if it's a boy I'll dream the policemen from Gauteng are chasing me, the Boers with red eyes and black hats and black boots. I think this was because when you are pregnant with a boy, you know he will kick you one day. He can't love you like a girl loves her mother. After Alexis died I used to dream like that, and I knew I was supposed to be pregnant – but because of the prayers of my mother I didn't get pregnant, not even one time.

Manraile, also, she didn't get pregnant before she was married. She was in school in 1975; she was seventeen years old. A policeman saw her walking in the street, and he asked the boys, 'Who is that lady? Where is she staying? Where does she come from?'

They told him she is staying in Mafikeng; she comes from the mountains.

One day when I was at home, visiting my children from working at Mrs Masongo's house, Manraile says, "*M'e*, there are visitors who are going to come here.'

I ask from where.

She says, 'You will see, and you will ask them.'

So in a short time two men come to my mother's house, greet us, and we invite them to sit down inside. They say, 'We are here about your daughter. Our son wants to marry her.'

I go outside to find Manraile. I find her outside listening, and I ask her if she knows this boy. She says, 'Yes, I know him.'

I say, 'These men are here, coming from Mafefoane, because the boy says he wants to marry you.'

She says Yes. She knows everything. She wants to marry him.

I go back inside the house and tell the men everything is fine. She knows the boy. So they say thanks, and we talk for a little while, and they go. One day again we find a letter that they want to come and pay *lobola*, and they are in a hurry because the man who will be her husband has to go to Qacha's Nek for his work, and he wants to go with a wife.

So they bring two cows, sixty sheep, and four hundred rands. At that time that was a lot of money. We sit down and have a talk, and we call these cows and sheep and money the same as eleven cows. I borrow the kraals of other people to put the animals in, and I agree. With this *lobola* I build the house I am still living in, a stone one.

The first time I saw Manraile's husband was at the wedding. I saw that he was a dark-skinned man with a big nose. That was all I could see; I had no feeling about him, good or bad. But I felt *ho lokile*, if she is happy, it's fine. We had a small feast; we killed only one sheep. Many people came, both from Mafikeng and from Mafefoane. I met his family, who had a little bit more than me because they owned a café. They seemed to be good people, and I could see that his mother was going to be nice to Manraile, so I was trying not to look sad. I smiled to everyone and greeted them, but my heart was not there.

After the feast, the same day, Manraile went to Mafefoane with her new family. I was heavy with sadness, because I know that marriage is very hard. I was fearing many things: my child is going to be poor, like me. She is going to work in other people's houses. I did not cry, but my heart was sore from thinking these things. My only daughter was getting married, but we had not many clothes for her. They will laugh at her in Mafefoane, I thought, because she has no nice things to wear. I looked at her in her little dress that was not much of a wedding dress, and I saw that she was poor almost all of her life, and she was going to be poor always. I was worried for her. I was still sleeping at the house of my friend, 'M'e 'M'ampho, because there was not room for me to sleep at my mother's house. The four boys were sleeping with my mother in the rondavel, and I knew it would be good to use that *lobola* to build a house so we could all sleep together. I should be happy for the *lobola* of Manraile, but I could not sleep well at all, because I love her and I can see her life is too hard, and marriage is hard.

I didn't want her to stay unmarried, because I knew she would have children, and if she has a husband he can help to support the children, so it's better. If she has no husband, she has to support the children alone, and that's hard; but sometimes I think marriage is harder than being alone. I didn't want her to be a nun, because if she was a nun they would send her far away from me, and I would miss her. And I didn't want her to be married, because marriage is hard. Many men sit home with no work, and they drink *joala*; they fight and argue, and there is no peace in the house. Others find work away from home and get new wives, and eat all the money, send nothing home to help the women in Lesotho. Then when the men do come home, they drink *joala* and fight; it is trouble, really. Some women marry rich men, which is good for them for a little while, but even a rich man is trouble. Rich men forget God, and rich men have many women, and they can be cruel. So I know that the life of women is hard, and there is no relief for that.

After Manraile's wedding, it took only three months to build my new house, and it was finished. We brought the stones down from the mountains, and that took time. Motlatsi and Ralibuseng helped me. When the new house was finished, we kept the old rondavel and we had two houses. I was very happy with the new house. We made a fire in the rondavel and I thanked God for helping me at last to have a house.

CHAPTER 14

My Father Died Laughing

My father was not a Christian like my mother. He was going to church when he met my mother, but the church was not very important to him. When he went to Gauteng, he forgot his prayers totally, and when we came to him in 1938 he was not a Christian at all. When she would pray, he would say, 'This Christian! I'm tired of this. Always praying.'

But one night that changed. We slept well, but in the middle of the night my mother woke up. She said she was dreaming, and she heard a voice call to her, 'Valeria, Valeria, wake up and pray. What is coming is bad.'

When she opened the curtain of the window she found that it's dark and lightning, very bad. She woke up and took her crucifix (I still have it at my house); she put it on the table and took two candles and put them beside the crucifix, and she prayed. She said to my father, 'Wake up and pray!'

He said 'No.' He was sleeping. He just rolled over and pulled the blanket over his head. I was very tired, and when I heard my mother say this, I opened my eyes a little bit, but I didn't move.

She was praying, praying, praying. Then there comes the lightning right inside the house, ZAM! The lightning came inside the house and went up the chimney, and some of the bricks of the chimney fell down inside. The candles went out. The house went black. The whole house was black, but the chest of Jesus on the crucifix was burning brightly like a light. When that happened, my father woke up, jumped out of bed, went down on his knees, and began to pray: 'Hail Mary, Mother of Jesus, help me! Molimo . . .' He said all the words he could think of from church. He didn't know how to pray, but he was praying all the Christian words he knew.

My mother was still praying, praying quietly. She didn't move. When the storm passed, she put her candles away and said, 'Now the lightning is gone. We can sleep.'

She slept. But my father and I didn't sleep that whole night. We were awake and afraid. We were not like her.

In the morning my father went to the *sangoma*. The *sangoma* told him, 'I see you have got a nice person in your house who helps you. It's a lady who holds a – I don't know what to call it. I see her, she is holding beads.'

'It's a rosary,' my father says.

'Oh!' says the *sangoma*. 'You call it a ro-what?'

'A rosary.'

'A rosary. I see. Are you a *Moroma*?' *Moroma* is the word we use for Roman Catholic.

My father says, 'Yes.'

The *sangoma* says, 'You were going to die, the whole of you in that house, but this lady saved you with her prayers.'

My father asks, 'Where does this lightning come from?'

'It was sent by a lady who was renting a room from *Ntate*. But he told her to pack her things and go out. So she was angry. This lady thought she could send a lightning to burn down the whole house, all six rooms. But God refused to kill you because of your wife's prayers.'

So after that, my father never said bad things about my mother's prayers. He came to listen to her, and he himself was baptised and made his first Holy Communion. After that, he says to my mother, 'You! You are a wizard.'

My mother says, 'Yes. I'm a wizard of God. You can't do me anything if God does not want.'

Then in 1949, at the same time that I went to Marakabei with Alexis, my mother came to Mafikeng, in the Roma Valley, to find a house. It was no more good to us, being in Gauteng. Benoni was too crowded, and the Boers were changing the laws and making life worse for all the black people, so many Basotho who were working there decided to go home. My mother said she would send for my father when she found a place to live. The Chief of Mafikeng gave my mother a rondavel, a small one, on the land where I live now. At first she could only borrow that house, but in time she was able to buy it; she paid ten rands, at that time we called it five pounds.

So when my father came from Benoni, he found my mother staying there, and he came to stay with her. My father started looking after sheep and cows when he arrived in Mafikeng, because there was no other work for a man who had only one leg. He was still sewing hats with crochet needles, as he did in Gauteng; but not so many people in Mafikeng had money to buy hats, so he also looked after other people's animals. But before long, he was accidentally murdered. This is what happened.

One day when he was going out to *naheng*, the open fields for grazing, with some sheep, the rain came. He left the sheep with some big boys, sixteen or fifteen years old, and he told them he will come back when the rain stops. Few minutes later one of these boys comes to his house, and *Ntate* Johannes says, 'What do you want now? It's still raining.'

The boy points a rifle at my father and says, 'I'm going to shoot you, *Ntate*.'

Ntate says, 'No, you can't shoot me, my boy.' And he laughs. He knows the boy is teasing. He looks down at the boy's muddy feet.

The boy says, 'I will shoot you, *Ntate*,' and he points the rifle at my father's head, and he shoots him. My father never even looked up. He died, smiling at this boy's feet.

After *Ntate* falls down, the boy runs away. He goes in the back of the house, running, afraid, and then he comes back and shakes *Ntate* and says, '*Ntate* Johannes, *Ntate* Johannes!' But my father is no more.

The boy runs away again in back of the house and comes back again, asking for help. The people nearby are drinking *joala* and don't hear. The boy comes again and tells one of the ladies, says, 'Come and see *Ntate* Johannes!' When the lady comes, she finds *Ntate* Johannes dead near the door.

She says, '*Ntate* was here. We were just talking with him here. But he is dead now. How can this be?'

The boy is crying. He doesn't run away. He just stands there and tells the people what happened. They take him to the police station and the boy tells again what happened. They take *Ntate* to the mortuary, and they ask the boy time and time again to tell what happened. And the boy still talks true.

The boy says he didn't know that this gun would work, because it was cold. He took the gun because he was going to shoot birds. So they go, they shoot the whole day, but this gun didn't work. So he thought that it was not well, the gun, or it can't shoot. But maybe because he put the gun in his blankets, it got warm. Suddenly it works. He was only playing with *Ntate*. He says, 'I didn't want to kill *Ntate* Johannes; he was my friend. I told him to leave the sheep; I would look after them. How can I kill him now?'

So my father was buried. My mother had no money for a proper funeral, and she had no way to send a message to tell me what happened. One day a boy from Roma came to Marakabei where I was working in the fields with many other people. He was gossiping, telling the people that a man in Roma who had only one leg was shot by a herdboy. An old lady who was listening told him, 'Hush! You are talking about the father of 'M'atsepo, who is working over there. Don't let her hear of it this way.'

The boy was shocked. He said, 'She is the daughter of *Ntate* Johannes, the man with one leg?'

The old lady told him Yes, so he must be quiet, and she came to me. I was working. I didn't hear anything. She told me she got a message that somebody wants me at home, and she said she will walk with me to 'M'anthunya's house, where I was living. On the way, she asked me many questions about my father.

'When did your father go to Gauteng?'

I tell her.

'When did he come home to Lesotho?'

I tell her.

'And how many children had your father?'

I say, 'Two: only me and my brother, Sephefu.' I wonder why she is asking me all these questions, but I didn't guess the reason at all.

When we arrive at 'M'anthunya's house, the old lady tells me that the boy from Roma told them that my father passed away last week. A boy shot him with a gun.

I was surprised, but I didn't know how to cry. I just said, 'What has happened has happened. What can I say? But I want to go home to see my mother.'

So the next day I go with 'M'anthunya, walking to Roma. When we arrive we find my father was buried yesterday. My mother was wearing a black dress, and she was very upset, because she loved *Ntate*.

When he was buried the police asked my mother,

'Can we put this child in jail or what?'

My mother says, 'No.' She says, 'I don't find how you can put him in jail, because I have been praying, and I see that this child is small, and he was only playing. He didn't mean to kill *Ntate* Johannes. For me, I say you should not put him in jail. But this is not the answer; you must not ask me only. Here in Mafikeng it's my home; people know me here. But maybe the people of Mokhokhong, where *Ntate* Johannes comes from, maybe they will think that I like this boy, maybe they will think shameful things about me unless I ask you to put the boy in jail. So I say you can do anything you like to do with him.'

The police say, 'Oh, 'M'e. He'll be one month in jail. After that, he must pay you ten cows for the life of your husband, so that your family may rest in peace.'

I don't think the family of that boy have paid those ten cows to this day. I think they have just brought only one cow. The boy went to Gauteng for a while to work, but when he was working he said he always saw my father in his dreams. My father said to him, 'Look at my wife. How poor she is. She has nothing to eat, nothing to wear.'

This dream comes again and again, so this makes the man mad. When he thinks of going to sleep he knows my father will come to him. So he is afraid to sleep. So he loses his work in Gauteng and he comes back to Lesotho.

One day my cousin sees him and says, 'Why didn't you tell me you were back in Lesotho?'

He says he was afraid.

'You know, I don't want even to pass by this house, because when I pass here I always get ashamed when I see 'M'e Lillane. I remember the father of Mpho when he talks to me he says "Look at my wife, how poor she is."'

My cousin says, 'I am going to tell *Rakhali*, my auntie, and you know my auntie is going to pray for you. Really, she is no more angry.'

He says, 'I didn't know.'

So my cousin goes to my mother and tells her the story of this boy.

My mother sends for this boy and says to him, 'Oh shame, Boy, I will pray for you. I will tell *Ntate* Johannes that he must go away from you, so you can work. He must not be always after you. I know you were just playing.'

So *Ntate* went away, and my mother one day asked this boy, 'Do you still see *Ntate* Johannes in your dreams?'

He says, 'No *'M'e*. He is no more coming, and I am working nicely.'

My mother says, 'Yes, I can always talk with people who are dead. I'm not afraid of these *balimo*. Even when I can see them, I don't care. I will talk to them. And they will listen. They will answer me if I want an answer, if I ask them a question.'

I can't do that. I can't speak with a person who is dead. Sometimes I see them in dreams. I used to see my mother, and I know if I see my mother there must be some woman who is going to pass away, or who passed away. My mother comes to talk with me sometimes in dreams, and I am glad to talk with her that way.

CHAPTER **15**

The Murderer in the Family

Alexis's brother Joseph is a cruel man and a murderer. Now he and I are the only elders left alive in the family, and I am supposed to meet with him to discuss family problems, but I cannot talk with the man who killed my children. The family is sad about this, but I know what I know. I told Joseph not to come in my house since 1989. I know that by our custom he is the father of all those children who are named Nthunya, but I don't want him in my house. Since he has not been in my house, these past four years are better.

Sometimes he passes my niece Nthabiseng's house. She asks him why he doesn't go to visit me. He makes up a story, maybe he says he is in a hurry, or he has other things to do. He used to beg money from me for a taxi, but I don't give him anything now. My heart takes time to turn away from someone, and then it takes time again to forgive. Usually after a few days I forget everything. But for Joseph it is taking longer.

The trouble started even before Alexis died, when I would go to Roma to visit Alexis in the hospital, taking the babies with me and leaving my boys in the mountains with Joseph. In July the water was frozen in the streams. This Joseph would wake up early. We were staying near the stream, and there was a dam by the stream. He took my children and a washing basin. He took a big stick to break the ice, and he put the ice-cold water in the basin, and he forced the children to wash in the icy water. He would not touch the water to wash himself, but he made them wash. If they didn't wash, he would beat them with a big stick.

Neighbours saw him and asked why he does this to the children. Joseph says nothing. He washes my children with ice

86

water until they are shivering and shaking. Then he brings them back to my house and tells them, 'Sit down near the fire.'

So when they sit by the fire, the children are shivering hard, and they get very sick. Then Joseph sends them out to watch the cattle, with nothing to wear but their little thin blankets in that cold and snow. My boys were sick; they fell asleep; and some of the sheep got away. When the children woke up and saw what had happened, they were afraid to come home. They know he will beat them. They sleep in the field, and he goes to fetch them. Some sheep will come home. Others will be lost. He says it is my fault: I have taught my children badly. Men always blame the women.

One time they were sleeping in the field, and they didn't eat for two days. When they came back in the evening of the third day, they were very hungry. This Joseph made a fire in the rondavel with wet dung, which makes big smoke. So he says these children must stay in the rondavel with the smoke. He closes the doors and windows and sits outside near the door. He wants to see how much he can torture them, just because he can. There is no one to stop him; I am in Roma, and he can do as he likes with these boys. One woman passes by and asks, 'Oh, you have made a big fire!'

He smiles to her and says, 'Yes! Because I want those children when they come home to find a big fire.'

'They are not yet home?'

He says, 'No.'

But the children are in the house: Tseliso, Motlatsi, Sello, Pakiso. Four children.

The children say they could hear *Ntate* Joseph talking with that lady. The smoke was choking them, but they took their blankets and covered their faces and crouched down to the floor until the smoke died out. God helped them.

When Joseph saw that it was dark, he opened the door. Then he says, 'You are still alive?'

The children say, '*E Ntate,*' Yes, father. They don't know what they can say.

He says, 'Take care. I will kill you.' But for that day they survived. He was always cruel; sometimes the children told me these things, and sometimes he told me himself. He would boast about how cruel he was with my children, because he knew it frightened me. He found he could be cruel to them and to me at the same time, and it pleased him to do this. Maybe it was a way for him to feel powerful. I was always thinking, 'My God, are my children still alive?'

Joseph says he can take a six-inch nail and drive it straight into the top of the head of my child. He says this smiling, looking at me, and touching the head of my child. He says in a soft voice, 'After that I can take another nail, and hammer it in with a hammer, and another one and another one till they come out the child's neck, here,' and he touches my child's neck, gently. He laughs, and I say nothing. After that, when he wants to scare me, he will just touch the tops of their heads. He says if he kills them this way, nobody can see how they died – no bleeding, no nothing, but the child will be dead. I watch his face when he talks like this, and I see it makes him happy to frighten me, so I try to look like I don't feel anything.

I have no choice. I must leave my boys with this man when I go to Roma. It is their home, and it is their job to watch the animals. But all the time I was in Roma, my heart would pound hard like a *sangoma*'s drum when I see a man riding toward me on a horse. I was afraid he was coming to tell me that one of my children was dead.

Before we all lived in the mountains together, Joseph worked in Gauteng for some years, in the mines. He married a woman in South Africa, and many times he beat her. One day he beat her so badly she got fed up. She went to the police and said, 'That man wants to kill me. He is a murderer; he is not afraid to kill people. If he kills me I will not be the first. Do you remember that a person was murdered last year on the road? It was Joseph who killed him, and you will find the gun under the wardrobe.'

So the police go, find him. They say, 'Give us the gun.'

Joseph growls like a dog, 'I have no gun.'

It was the Boer police. They hit him. 'Bring the gun!' They know where is the gun. They find it under the wardrobe. They take him to the jail and he was there for five years. And the jail is where they taught him to do these murders with nails and other things too horrible to speak about. He came out of jail meaner and crueller than he was before.

Every day when I was not at home I worried about my children. One day when I come from work, I find Motlatsi and Tseliso at my mother's home. Their feet were swollen badly because they walked all the way from Marakabei to Roma. So I asked them, 'How did you come to be here?'

Tseliso says, 'Two nights ago, before I slept I told Motlatsi, "When I wake you up in the morning, you must wake up quickly and we can go to Roma." So we didn't sleep. Early in the morning, just at the beginning of dawn, we go. One man saw us, a neighbour. He was glad to see us running away, because everybody in the village was tired of seeing *Ntate* hitting us like dogs and threatening to kill us every day.

'The neighbour man whispers, "Where are you going?"

'I say, "We want to go to Roma, to our mother."

'The man says, "You must be quick so when Joseph wakes up he finds you far away."

'We go.'

Later Tseliso found out what happened when *Ntate* Joseph woke up.

He came to the door. 'Tseliso! Tseliso!' he calls. 'Motlatsi! Sello!' He wakes up Sello with a whip. But Sello doesn't know where the boys are. Sello pulls his little torn blanket around him, to hide from that whip, and he says, 'I don't know where they are.'

Ntate shouts at Sello, 'You know!' and he beats him with the whip, and kicks him on the ground.

Sello with his big round eyes cries out, 'It's true, *Ntate*, I don't know where they are.'

Ntate leaves Sello on the ground and goes to that neighbour who saw the boys leaving. The neighbour says, 'I didn't see any of your boys.'

Ntate says, 'Maybe they are running away to their mother in Roma. Let me borrow a horse.'

This man says, 'No. I'll ride it and go and fetch them. You go that way. I'll go towards Roma.' He knows if he can find them he will put them on the horse and help them.

When he was on top of a mountain he saw the boys, far away.

He just sat down on that mountain and let the horse graze. He watched the boys, and he sat there till sunset. At sunset he went back and said to Joseph,

'I have travelled all day, but I didn't see them, totally.'

And that's how they got away. They slept at Nyakosoba; it's more than half the way to Roma. If they sleep there, they can get to Roma by ten in the morning.

They find my mother. She was very glad to see the children, even with their small blankets, walking by foot, with no shoes. When I came home from Mrs Masongo's house I found them. I was glad and sorry at the same time. I boil the water and wash their feet and put much Vaseline on those sore feet of theirs. And the next day I gave my mother ten shillings to go and buy them some clothes. She found trousers for two shillings, and shirts for two shillings, at St. Theresa's Mission.

But in time Joseph came to Roma, looking for them, and he was very angry. He tried to threaten them, 'If you stay with your mother, you will die.'

They didn't listen to him. They knew if they go back to the mountains with him, they will die, so maybe they have a chance if they live with me. So then Joseph put Basotho medicine on my family. We knew he did that, because he wanted to kill us.

But when a person puts this kind of medicine on people, he must take care or it will come back to him. Joseph was already talking to himself when he was alone. He was not sleeping well. And he got a warning. Some of his friends took him to a *sangoma*. The *sangoma* said, 'You have put bad medicine on the family of your brother, and now this medicine begins to come back to you. If you don't stop this, you are going to go mad before you die.'

So he asked the *sangoma* what he must do to save himself. The *sangoma* told him, 'You must call all the children of Alexis, and the wife of Alexis, and make a feast. It can be a sheep or a goat. Take the gall-bladder of this animal and put it in a basin of water, and ask those children to wash you with this water. You must tell them what you have done and beg forgiveness.'

Joseph told the *sangoma*, 'Yes, I will do this.'

In December, near to Christmas, he came to me and asked me to send my children to him for a feast. He said, 'I know you are working, so you can't come.' He never asked me to come. He wanted my children only. But they refused.

I tell them, 'Your uncle says you must go to the mountains. He makes a feast.' They say 'No.' They refuse. They only go back with me, when I go after I bury Alexis. Then I return to the mountains with these boys, and they go back to taking care of what is left of our sheep and looking after Joseph's sheep and cows. For a time I am not sure what to do. Alexis's father says I must go to Roma and go back to work for Mrs Masongo so that the children can go to school and have something to eat. Joseph says, 'No! She must stay here and look after the cows and the sheep. We need the children here, to work with us.'

But their grandfather said, 'You can keep the sheep. They are few, and you can take them for yours now. But this woman will take just one cow and ten sheep so she can buy a blanket to wear and find work.'

Before we can go to Roma we have to get a paper from the Chief that says, 'This cow belongs to 'M'atsepo Nthunya, and she can sell it if she wants.'

So *Ntate* sends Joseph with the cow to get the paper. On the way Joseph finds a lady who says, 'I like this cow. I want to buy it.'

He says 'M'atsepo is going to sell it, but first I must get a paper from the chief.

She tells him, 'Leave the cow here. Go get the paper. Tomorrow I will give you the money.'

He says, 'No, I will take the cow with me.'

But she warns him, 'This cow will be tired, going up and down, and then it will not be worth as much to me. You cannot do this to the cow. Leave it here.'

He says, 'No! I will come with the cow tomorrow. I want the Chief to know that I have done the right thing.'

So the lady says, 'OK, fine. But please bring me this cow tomorrow. I want to buy it.'

Joseph goes. He gets the paper. Puts the cow back in the kraal. Early in the morning the next day he goes to the kraal and takes dust from the ground and holds it to the cow's nose and suffocates the cow. He did it before with my sheep, and he did it again with that cow. Then he comes in the house. He says, '*Ntate, Ausi*, you know what? Ach! I don't like what's happened. Somebody has killed that cow of 'M'atsepo's.'

We listen, looking at him. I find I am not even surprised. I answer, 'Yes, somebody did. And I know who it was.'

'How do you know, *Ausi*, did you see?'

When I start to answer, *Ntate* says, 'Shut up, 'M'atsepo. Don't answer this boy, because he has killed the cow. He thought we can't go to Roma if the cow is dead. We don't mind. We are going. He will eat the cow's meat. We don't care. We are going now. Take the children, put them on your back, and let's go.'

Joseph was ashamed when he saw that *Ntate* and I don't care. I don't shout, I don't say anything because *Ntate* says, 'Don't talk to this devil. I don't like this man, even if he is my own son.' We leave Joseph alone in the mountains with a dead cow and no boys to use for donkeys, and he is very angry.

We drove our ten sheep and two goats when we went. People on the way bought the two goats and we came with the sheep to Roma. We sold all but one sheep; we leave that one for me to make a feast for the end of mourning Alexis; and we start our new life in Roma. But Joseph was not finished with us. He had plenty of time to sit in the mountains and plan his revenge.

He started with me. One day I had a pain in my throat, and I had a pain in my stomach as if I had eaten something bad. I felt like vomiting, but I didn't vomit. I let it pass. I sleep, I wake up. I go to work for Mrs Masongo, but I know I have something wrong in my body. I have a little bit of cramps in my stomach. Then I got a headache across the whole top of my head so bad I put my head in my hands. I can't see. So I go to a *sangoma* who gives me medicine to sniff like snuff. I take it. I feel a little bit better in the head. But my stomach was still in pain, pain, pain. From there I am coughing, vomiting, coughing, vomiting. The *sangoma* gave me some medicine again and told me I have eaten something bad in a dream. She says some person gave me this bad food in a dream.

The *sangoma* says, 'This person wants you to die so he can be able to make these children work for him. Because one day after the children left the mountains to stay with you, you said, "Nobody can take my children until the day I die."

'When you said that, you gave him an idea. When you are dead he is the only person who can take charge of these boys. Now he wants you to die so he can get these boys to go to Gauteng and work for him, call him their father, and make him rich. So he wants to kill you by this medicine when you sleep.'

The *sangoma* gave me medicine and I drink, drink, drink. I mix with red pepper and it eats this thing which is in my stomach. I mix red chilli pepper with ginger ale, hot, and drink, so the stomach will be better.

The medicine made me a little bit better, but I kept getting sick again and again, because the medicine of Joseph is very strong. One day I was in so much pain I had to lie down near Mrs Masongo's house. I asked who can help me. This thing inside goes up and down. A man who worked at the University found me and said, 'You should go up there in the mountains near Popanyane. You will find a person who can help you to vomit this thing out.'

So I went there. I woke up early in the morning on Sunday when I'm off. I was not knowing the place, but I ask people on the way. They show me this man's house. He gives me medicine in a clay pot and says, 'Drink.'

I drink very much medicine.

After that, 'Kneel down. Put your finger down your throat, and vomit.' So I do this, and the medicine comes out and the doctor takes the water that I have vomited and he takes a small straw broom and pours the water through the broom like a sieve. He found the skin of a snake there. He took it and put it in a basin of fresh water. He says, 'This is what was going up and down in your stomach. When it is in your stomach it is a snake, and it eats you. The person who put a spell on you took the skin of this snake and ground it to a powder and gave it to you in a dream.'

So that *sangoma* took this thing and buried it in the ground by his house.

I go home and tell my mother what happened, and my stomach got better. With God's help Joseph was not able to kill me. But then Joseph began his plan to kill Tseliso, Motlatsi, and Mofihli, and in time he found it easy to kill them. He had his ways to make it look like they died from other causes, so nobody can prove he did it, but I always knew the cause. It was Joseph who killed them.

CHAPTER 16

The Frozen Herdboy

When we were living in Marakabei, one winter day there was a heavy rain. Children were watching sheep in the mountain meadows, but it rained the whole day. One child, Sello, who was eight years old, didn't come home at sunset. Sello's parents were working in Gauteng, and he was working for Alexis's brother, Joseph, and staying with me. Sello was a shy, quiet boy and very gentle, with big round eyes that always looked like he just had a surprise. He seemed to be a bad-luck child; many bad things happened to him, and it was never his fault. So on this day of the storm, we wondered where is Sello. It was hailing, snowing, lightning, very bad storm, and the rivers were high. We thought he couldn't get home, because he was on the wrong side of the river. He had no clothes, only a small loincloth and the torn rags of a blanket.

Dark came, and I asked Joseph to go look for Sello, but he refused. He said, 'It's too late. It's dark. We can't see him.'

So we slept.

Next day, they go near the river and call him, 'Sello! Sello! Come home!'

No answer came.

So Joseph went to another man and asked him to go and help find Sello. They looked up and down, up and down, until they found him under a bush we called *lekhapu*, kneeling and curled up round like a bowl. He is freezing. His skin is turning white, like paper; his eyes are closed, he can't talk, but the two men lean close and find he is breathing. They touch him, and his bones are cold and stiff, like a dead person. He can't move. They carry him on their shoulders like a frozen lamb, and they go to the stream, not the river which is swollen wide. At the stream, which is full up, one man crosses and stands. The other one throws Sello across the stream as if he is a sheepskin. They almost drop him in the water, when the man who is supposed to catch him misses and just grabs him by the ankle. Sello's head hits some stones, but he makes no sound and he doesn't bleed. They pull him away from the stream and put him on their shoulders again and go home.

When they arrive at home I see that he is almost dead. I boil the milk and try to feed him with a spoon. His teeth are shut tight like a clamp. I take the Vaseline and rub it all over his body. I make a big fire and put him to sleep in the same room with the fire, but not too close to the fire, because I know if he is too close to the fire he will die. I put many blankets on him, with sheepskins on top.

So the next day he was better when we woke up, but he didn't go to the grazing-land that day because he was still weak; he could hardly walk. He began to move his hands and feet, and his skin came back to his colour, not white any more. And after two days Joseph said he must go again to watch the sheep. I could see Sello was afraid, but he didn't say anything. He just looks out at the *naheng* with those surprised eyes, takes his little scrap of blanket, and goes.

Every day when he goes to the mountains we fear he won't be coming back, because he was always afraid he might lose an animal. If an animal disappears, the child hides, because he knows he is going to be punished like a dog. So when he goes to the mountains we look after him. After dinner we go check him and call his name, tell him that it's time to come home. He must bring the sheep home at four.

He was staying with me for a few years, and he was like one of my own children, only I worried for him more, because he always seemed afraid. He didn't play like the other boys. Every day he went to the *naheng*, and when he came home he was just watching, watching everything with those big eyes.

When Alexis came home I told him how cruel Joseph is to Sello.

Alexis says, 'I know. He does everything bad to Sello because he is not his child, so he doesn't care what happens to him. Sello's father is working in Gauteng. If Sello dies, it is less than if one of Joseph's dogs dies in the field.'

So there was nothing we could do to help Sello.

When he was nine, the mother of his mother came to fetch him. She lived in Leribe, and she took him home with her. At first Joseph was refusing. He said, 'No. He can't go without his father's word.'

But the father of Alexis says, 'It's not your business. It's not your child. You want to make him a donkey all the time, to do your work for nothing. You must let his granny take him.'

My heart hurt when he left. I never saw him again after that day, but I heard that first he went with his grandmother to Leribe. When he grew to be sixteen, he went to his mother and father in Gauteng. So when he was there a very short time, maybe just some weeks, until he got his first pay, they say he was coming from work and the *tsotsis* caught him. They took his money and cut his neck with a knife, and they put him on the train tracks. But when the train comes, the trainmen see there is a person lying on the tracks. So they stop and they take him away. In the morning his mother and father were told to go and see if they can know the boy. They found it was Sello, dead. When his father came to Lesotho to visit, long after Sello died, he told me how it happened.

CHAPTER 17

The Snow Was So Cold
It Was Blue

I know it is true that people who are sick for a long time can tell you when they are going to die. Alexis knew, right to the very hour. Once he knew his time it was not hard for us; it was the time before he knew that was hard. But 'M'anthunya's death was a surprise to everyone.

In August 1961, I got another baby boy. I named him Ralibuseng, which was my father-in-law's name. He was born at my mother's home in Mafikeng, in the Roma Valley. He came too fast for me to get to the hospital, but he was fat and healthy. I stayed with my mother until he was three months old, and then I began to pack my things to go home to the Maluti.

Before I could leave my mother's house, my mother-in-law, 'M'anthunya arrived. She came to say 'Hello' to me, and to see the baby. We slept together, and she told me that I should hurry home to look after the children, because she was on her way to Maseru to find work, and there was no one home to do the cooking or look after the house. She said they were ploughing, but they had nothing to plough. There was no food in the fields that year. There was nothing to eat. That was why she had to go try to find work in Maseru.

I just took only two weeks and found myself at home with Ralibuseng on my back. The day I came home I got a message that 'M'anthunya had passed away. I could not believe it at first. They said she was sick for two days only, and then she passed. It was a shock to us, and it was a time for me to see that everything was up to me. So quickly, with no preparation, I became the woman at the head of the family.

My father-in-law went down to Maseru to bury her, but there was no funeral. We couldn't go, because it was raining. The rivers were full, and nobody could walk through them with a small child. I sat in the house, watching the rain fall, and thinking many things. Alexis was the first son, so now I had to take care of all the children and the fields. My father-in-law was like another child. He couldn't do anything for himself.

I stayed in my little rondavel and left the sister and brothers of Alexis in the big house with the old man, but they all came to me for food. It was a hard time, because it was true what 'M'anthunya said to me in Roma: there was no food. There was one girl in the house, but she was too young to cook. I had four children; Alexis had two brothers still at home and one sister. Seven children, two men, and me.

For three more years we struggled. Alexis brought money home when he could. The fields improved. The sheep increased. Slowly we came to feel safe from hunger again, and then, in August 1964, I got another baby boy. For this one I stayed in the Maluti, because the family could not keep going if I went home to have my baby properly. I asked an old lady living near to my house to help me for a few days. She knew how to cut the cord and do what was necessary when the baby came.

This baby was Mofihli, born 16 August 1964, while the snow was falling. There was a heavy snow that year, snow up to my hips if I walked outside. There was so much snow it was blue. When you lift your foot out of the snow, the hollow place looks blue. It was that cold. It was the same snow that brought the cold into Alexis's bones.

Alexis was driving a tractor with a snow plough in the mountains, clearing the road to the Katse Dam they were building. We called it Letsie Ledrai at that time. He had a blanket around his waist and over his legs, but it was not enough. He got cold inside his legs. At the end of the month he came home and said, 'The snow was falling on my legs, and my legs have started to be sore.'

He told me to help him put his feet in a basin of hot water before he went to bed, and I rubbed his legs with a medicine he brought home. It was a smelly yellow medicine, like Vaseline. I rubbed it into his legs and wrapped his legs in big heavy socks. He arrived home on a Thursday. On Sunday he went back to work.

He worked on the snow plough again, but in only two weeks they sent him to Maseru, to the hospital. As soon as I find a letter that he is in hospital, I go right away to see him. I left the older children with Alexis's brother and took the little ones to my mother in Roma. I took only the baby on my back, and I walked to Lithabaneng, on the road to Maseru. There I found some of 'M'anthunya's relatives, and they let me spend the night; the next day I walked on into Maseru.

Alexis was in a big room with many men; they called it Ward Five. They have bandaged him in cotton wool, from his feet to his hips. He said he was feeling a little bit better. He stayed in hospital six weeks. I used to go visit him every Friday and Saturday. On Sunday I would walk back to Roma to take care of the children.

After six weeks, Alexis came out of hospital and went to Lithabaneng for a week; then he went back to work. It was no more cold, but his body was feeling cold. It was October; it was spring. But he was cold, and I worried about that. Nothing would make him warm. He said the cold was deep in the bones of his legs.

I went home to the Maluti to look after all the children, the sheep and goats, and everything. I was also working in the fields, hoeing and trying to help the crops to grow. I was cooking and washing for everybody. And while I was working, I was wondering why Alexis was still cold. He would come home at the end of every month, but he was always not well. His kidneys bothered him. When he tried to lift a heavy thing, he would be in pain.

We need the money, so he has to go to work, all summer and autumn. But then comes another winter, 1965. In August he cannot move his legs from the cold. He went to hospital again, and I was two months pregnant. He told me he wanted to work, so he can help us with money, and he tried to work even when his legs were hurting. So he worked and he worked until one day he fell where he was standing. His legs would not hold him. There was nothing, he said. No feeling in them. It was like he had no legs at all. Nothing underneath him. A man working beside him tried to pick him up and asked, 'Why did you fall?'

Alexis said he didn't know.

So from that day he was not going to work again, ever. Those legs were not going anywhere. Men from his job brought him to the hospital, and at the hospital they started to treat him, and they sent me a message that he was there.

Again I took the small children to my mother and began to walk to Maseru every week to visit Alexis. I took Manraile with me, and Mofihli on my back. Alexis was afraid I would lose the baby, so he said I should stay with the relatives in Lithabaneng, and not go back and forth to Roma. But when you stay with relatives, you have to buy food for the whole family and take food to the person who is sick. I was too poor; I could not buy all this food. So I would take one whole day, walking from Roma to Lithabaneng. I would sleep at Lithabaneng, and then walk half the day to Maseru. After visiting Alexis, I would walk back to Lithabaneng and sleep again; and the next day walk home to Roma.

I tried to find work, to earn some money while I was in Roma, but it was hard to find work because I was pregnant. Manraile was eight years old, and we were both very strong, so we fell into a kind of pattern of walking to Maseru every week, and soon it felt like it was our life to do this. We would take *motoho*, a sour porridge drink, in a canteen; and *papa* and *moroho* in a cake tin. Sometimes there would be water on the way; sometimes no water. Manraile had no shoes. I had some old shoes that were falling apart, but they still had a little bit of sole to protect my feet from the stones, so I was a little bit better off.

Alexis was in Ward Five again. His legs were very big and wrapped in cotton wool. He said, 'I can't see how I can ever use these legs again,' and he was very sad. 'What am I going to do for you and the children?'

They gave him a wheelchair, so he could move around in the hospital, but he could see that he was not ever going to leave that place. He could not move with a wheelchair in the mountains. He could not even go anywhere in Roma, or Maseru. There were not so many roads then, and no sidewalks. A wheelchair was useless except in the hospital.

So when it was almost time for the baby to come, I went back to the mountains. In February 1966, I got a baby boy, Muso. We named him Muso, which means Government, because he was born in the year of independence, and my father-in-law didn't have to pay tax to the British anymore. Before independence, every man, no matter how poor, had to pay tax to the British or he was put in jail. My father-in-law was glad not to pay tax anymore, so we named the baby Muso. But my heart was troubled because of Alexis. I stayed in the mountains for the harvest. 'M'anthabiseng came with me to help me have the baby, and she worked with me in the fields. It was a good year; we had plenty of sorghum and green split peas. We dried them and put them in big baskets.

Then I left Tseliso and Motlatsi in the mountains and I went back to Roma with Mofihli, Ralibuseng, Manraile, and with Muso on my back. I needed Manraile to help me with the little boys; there was no time for her to go to school. I came to be sorry for that. She didn't go to school until she was eleven, because I needed her help.

In Roma we stayed with my mother. My mother was living alone when I was in the mountains, and she was very happy to have us all with her. My mother always worried when we were in the mountains. She said she didn't like us to be there, because when we were hungry we were going to sleep with that hunger. It was half a day to the shop and half a day back, and no money to buy anything at the shop if we could get there.

As soon as we get back to Roma, I take only one day to rest and I go to hospital to see Alexis. I took only Muso and Manraile with me. Muso was nursing, and Manraile went along to help carry the baby. When we arrive at the hospital, it was the first time for Alexis to see Muso. Alexis cried tears, and he told the nurses, 'Look at my child. He finds me in the hospital with nothing to wear. Now I have no money to help my children. I worked many, many years, and now my boy finds me this way.'

The nurses were afraid of Alexis because he was sometimes very angry. He would shout at them and say he wants to go out and work for his children. But he was too sick. His legs would not work. And when the nurses saw him crying and holding his baby boy, they could not stay in the room. They covered their faces and went out.

Again I fall into the rhythm of walking to Maseru with Manraile. Muso on my back. There were very few cars in that time. Once a coal truck passed us, and the man driving the coal truck said, 'Look at this woman and these small children. I must give them a ride.'

So we got on top of the coal in the back of the truck. I hated that. It was windy and dirty there. It was my first time and I never did it again. We walked all the other times, until 1967. I go because it's right for me to go. If I didn't go, I would dream many bad dreams. It was hard, but I felt I must go. My mother felt the same thing. She was very sympathetic with Alexis. She was worried, because Alexis helped her many times. When we finished harvesting maize, he used to come with a donkey and give sacks of maize to my mother. When we slaughter a sheep, he brings her the meat. He liked her very much, so she also felt I must go to hospital to see him. One day I told Alexis that I was going home to the Maluti because it was time to plough.

He says, 'What are you going to do there for food, because I'm here? I don't want you to go back. I want you to stay here in Maseru and come to visit me.'

I say, 'What about your sheep and goats?' I was selling the sheep from the mountains. I would sell one or two at a time to get money for paraffin and maize meal. At that time you could get four rands for each sheep. One rand would be enough for a big bag of maize meal. But some of the sheep were stolen in the mountains.

When they started to steal, they took thirty sheep in one night. From there they took one animal every night. Tseliso was watching the animals by day, but the thieves took them at night. There was no one to stay up all the time and watch the animals, and we thought the thieves were many. No child alone could stop them. I didn't tell Alexis all of this, because he would worry too much, and there was nothing he could do.

He says, 'I told you to sell all the animals and bring the money to the bank, so you can help the children to go to school. Look at Manraile. She is going up and down with you because she has to carry the baby when you are tired. I don't like this. I want to get out of this hospital so I can help you.'

So one of the doctors said, 'Alexis, you must not go out of this hospital, because the government will no longer pay money for your treatment if you leave.' The doctor said that because he was hurt while he was working for the government, the government pays money for him each month he is in hospital, money for the family and money to pay the cost of the hospital.

It was my first time to hear this. The doctor tells me a cousin of Alexis who speaks very good English gets the money for our family, and I am supposed to go to him for the money. This cousin works in Maseru and he goes to the government to get the money for us.

So I go to that cousin. He says, 'Oh, this is not a good time to come for the money. Come next month.'

I go the next month and he says, 'There is no money this month. Come again next month.'

Every month it is the same way. In time I quit going to him, but I know he is taking Alexis's money, the money for our family. My mother tells me not to worry, because this cousin is rich. She says rich people are always like this: greedy. But she says God will bring him down in the end, and we should say nothing to him.

I notice that this man built himself a very nice house while Alexis is in hospital. I know he is building with our money. When this man sees me, even now, he always has shame. I know he kept our money. So all the time Alexis was sick, I had no money. My mother was working in people's gardens, and she made enough money to buy a little maize meal, some paraffin and soap. We ate *papa*, *moroho*, and peas from my fields. That is why I don't like peas now. I ate them too many years. I can't eat them any more.

So I keep going to see Alexis in the hospital. His legs were in bandages. I want to see the wounds, but the nurses tell me I cannot look at his legs, or I can be sick. They say the meat comes off his bones. He was getting weaker and weaker, and very sick. One day he told the nurses, 'I know that wife of mine has no money to come see me, but please telephone to the police station in Roma; tell her to come and see me, and bring Muso, because I am very sick and I want to see them one more time.'

When the police find me and give me this message, I borrow money for the bus so I can go to Maseru quickly. I take Muso on my back. I find Alexis in a special room alone, and he is very ill, in so much pain his face is gray and he is almost too weak to speak or move. He says to me, 'I'm sick, my wife, but I will help you all I can.'

He was very glad to see Muso. He ask me to give him the child. I lay Muso on the bed beside him, and he uses all the strength he has, to take the child and hold him to his heart. He says, 'Oh, my child, you are going to be poor.'

I cannot stand to see him feel so much pain of heart. I try to give him some hope. I say, 'Why? Because you are going to be well, and come out of this hospital, and you will be able to work again.'

I say that, but I know he is so sick, he can't be better. I think maybe I can take him home to die there. And as if he is reading my mind, he says, 'Yes. Tomorrow I want you to come with a *koloi* and take me home with you. I'm tired of this hospital. But be sure you come early, before nine o'clock.'

I tell him nine o'clock is too early. I can't go back to Roma, find a *koloi*, and bring someone back here with me that early, but he says, 'You must try, so that we can go home.'

Outside the room I find a nurse. I tell her I am going to Roma to try to find a person who has a *koloi*, to take Alexis home. She says No. She says Alexis is very sick; when they wash him, the meat goes away from his bones as if a dog has eaten him. We cannot move him from that bed. There is no going home for him now. She says I must prepare for his funeral.

I go back to Roma on the bus, and my heart is very sore. Alexis was in so much pain, and he was sick for such a long time, I think it can be better for him when he is dead. In my mind I see many times how he held Muso to his heart. I feel Muso move against my back, and I think about the nurse, telling me to prepare for the funeral. But I have no money to prepare.

At ten o'clock the next day a policeman comes to my door. He says he got a phone call to say that Alexis passed away at nine o'clock that morning. It was August 1968. Again I borrow money, again I go to Maseru. At the hospital they tell me, 'This person should not be taken home for burial. We know that you are alone; you have no one to help you. The government will help you to bury your husband here and will buy his coffin.'

So we buried him there, close to the hospital. You could not even call it a funeral. It was only me and his one brother and sister who lived in Lithabaneng. They let me sleep at their house many times when I was coming to see Alexis. Now they came with me for his burial. We took him straight from the hospital to the cemetery. There was no feast, no nothing. After that, I went home again to Roma.

I planned to go to the Maluti the next day, to tell Alexis's father. But in the morning before I left, Alexis's father arrived. Every day Radio Lesotho announces all the deaths from that day, and *Ntate* heard from the radio that Alexis died. He was too late for the funeral, or rather the burial. So I walked back to the Maluti with *Ntate*. We slept on the way, as always, and we arrived at home just as the sun was setting. It was always Alexis's favourite time to be in the mountains, to sit in front of our little rondavel and watch the sun set.

In the morning our neighbours came. I cut my hair and took all my clothes off and put on my old clothes that I had left behind when I went to Roma. I did not have money for black clothes. We stayed in the mountains August, September, and October. Then I came back to Roma again, with the last of the animals that had not been stolen: ten sheep, one cow, and one horse. I left all my things in the house as if I would be coming back. Left everything. Left the rondavel with a nice door. Just left it all there and went to work at the University, cleaning houses.

CHAPTER 18

Joseph Kills My Three Boys

While I was working for Mrs Masongo, Tseliso went to the gold-mines in the Republic. One day while he was there he saw Joseph, who was also working in the mines. Joseph was drinking, and he was very angry when he saw Tseliso. Joseph cursed him, '*Hei, Uena*! What are you doing here? This is work for men, but you don't like to work! You like to run behind your mother all the time; you are not a man. But I can tell you this: you are not going to see this mother of yours again. You will go home before your time, and you will go home dead, because you are going to die in the mine, under the ground.'

Joseph had very strong medicine, because the hate in him was so strong, and he almost made that curse come true. There was an accident in the mine, under the ground. Tseliso thought he was going to die, and when the rocks fell on him he remembered Joseph's deep voice, growling like a dog, 'You will go home dead, *uena.*'

But God helped Tseliso, so that Tseliso only had a broken leg. After the accident they put a piece of zinc in his leg, in a hospital in the Republic, and they sent him home with no money. They said he broke his contract when he broke his leg. He can only get the money at the end of a year, and if he breaks his leg before the year is up, he must go home with no money. When he came home he was walking all right, but he was hurting, and when it was cold he was hurting so badly in that leg, it reminded me of the pain Alexis had.

He brought with him only sixty rands and that piece of zinc inside his leg, after all that time, nearly a whole year. He says they call him a labourer, not a miner, which means they feed him, they give him a place to sleep with many other men; but there is no money unless he finishes the year. He has nothing – only one blanket and one trouser. So for a while he was staying at home, looking for piece jobs. Tseliso knew it was the curse of Joseph that made it so hard for him to find work.

One day Tseliso said, 'I'm going to beat Joseph.'

I said No. He mustn't. Joseph is his father, since his father is dead. Even if he is a devil, we have no right to beat him.

Tseliso says, 'These people can kill us because you have a forgiving heart, because you honour the old ways. You are too kind.'

I say, 'It's not true. Joseph will curse us no matter what we do. If we do what is wrong, if we hate him, we add to the curse because we bring more poison inside ourselves.'

For a long time this was a struggle for Tseliso. Then he got a job building houses.

He found a shy, gentle girl with large round eyes and a small boy-child working in the café near me. She was staying in the café, and they fell in love with each other. Her family was up in the Maluti, and her uncle says to her father, 'You must not tell these people to bring much *lobola* for this girl. She has a baby already. You must take three cows only for her.'

I say I cannot pay any *lobola*. I have nothing. I am working just for *papa*. Tseliso must make the money for this small *lobola* when he is back in the mines.

But he didn't go to the mines any more. He was sometimes a whole year without working. They began staying together, Tseliso and 'M'athuso, in 1978, when their first girl was born. They had a house which was given to 'M'athuso by her uncle, and she and Tseliso were staying there, close to my house. They had another child, Ntsoaki, in March 1980, and then a third girl, Libuseng, in 1983. 'M'athuso was still working at the café until 1990, and Tseliso would work sometimes and not work sometimes. Joseph was still working his medicine on Tseliso. He was not going to be finished until Tseliso was dead.

Tseliso spent all his time with his family when he was not working or sleeping at my house. He didn't like to go out with other men all the time, and he never saw other women, because he was so much in love with 'M'athuso. He loved his children very much and liked to play with them and bring them to me. He was good to me, very respectful always, and we were very close.

But I worried about him drinking. One day I told him, 'Because you are not working, I am going to take Ntsoaki to Mazenod to stay with your brother.' He was very upset. Ntsoaki looked just like him, and she was his favourite. If you saw a photo of him as a child, you would think it was Ntsoaki. He was even light-skinned like her before he started drinking. The drinking turned him pitch black. People used to say to Tseliso, 'This is your child; she is made only from you; we think she has no mother.' And he would smile, very pleased.

'Yes,' he would say, 'this is my child.' So when I say I will take Ntsoaki away, he says, 'Oh! my little girl who never talks. She just sits with me and listens to the quiet and feels how much I love her. When she's hungry she never says so. But you will take her to Ralibuseng because I'm not working.'

I say 'Yes, because you are not taking care of her. You are drinking *joala* all day, and when we arrive here we find you drunk, and no one is watching the child.'

Because he was not a person to answer back to me, he was quiet, and I took Ntsoaki to Mazenod. She stayed for three months. Then she was back again, because the wife of Ralibuseng says, 'She doesn't talk, is always quiet. I am afraid to keep her. When Ralibuseng talks to her, she talks, but she talks to him only. I think it's not good to keep her, because Ralibuseng favours her over his other children.' She was jealous of how much Ralibuseng loved Ntsoaki.

Tseliso was very, very glad to have Ntsoaki back. He says, 'I told you, *'M'e*, I don't want my child to go away. It's because I'm not working that you take my child away from me.'

It made me sad for him to say this. I say, 'It was not because you're not working. It's because you're drinking, and you don't go and look for work.'

When he was drinking he liked us to sing. He was always a happy someone when he was drinking, and he liked dancing. He would sing and dance and make everyone else happy, and then he would say, ''M'athuso, let's go to bed!' even if it was only six o'clock. He would sit down, and he would make her sit down. And he would talk and talk.

Sometimes he loved her too much. He would say, 'You are going out with other men. You don't care about me. I see men all the time wanting you.' But he doesn't hit her. He never hit anyone. He was a gentle person.

He keeps finding piece-work. Finally, in January 1987, he finds work building a small school on the campus. He works from January to May. It comes to be very cold, and he is building the lavatories and he gets very cold, gets a pain in the back of his shoulder. It was May. By June he passed away. The pain started in his shoulder, and he was always cold. We went to the university clinic and got some pills, but he was still cold. Coughing and shaking. We took him to the hospital in Maseru, but he didn't take even two weeks there, just a little over one week and he passed away.

Nobody was with him when he died. 'M'athuso came to see him from noon till two o'clock on that Sunday, and she found him very sick. The nurses say, 'This person was better in the morning, but now we don't know what is the matter.'

When 'M'athuso arrives at home we find a message that he passed away at three o'clock. He was just waiting to see her, and she says he was very happy to see her. But he passed when she left. I was very surprised, because I didn't think that he was so sick that he would die.

I was a member of Thusanang Burial Society, and I paid the dues for Tseliso, so they helped me to bury him. I had to buy a coffin, but they paid for the funeral. I took time off work for two weeks. *Ntate* Engels paid for a lady to work in my place for those two weeks. Tseliso was my first child who lived, my little man who carried heavy burdens even when he was a small thing; my favourite boy and the one I felt closest to. He was my most joyful child, and he always respected me. We never had hard words as many mothers and sons do. I cannot speak of the loss of that one, even now, except to know it was his time to see God.

After Tseliso died, Joseph started to work on Motlatsi. Motlatsi also went to the gold-mines in the Republic, and Joseph used to frighten Motlatsi in a dream which came many times. In the dream Joseph comes to him and growls deep in his throat like thunder in the mountains, 'Let's go home, *uena!*'

Joseph is on a horse and is pulling a small black dog on a rope behind him. He's got a green blanket, and he wears black trousers and black shoes. When he says, 'Let's go home,' Motlatsi will wake up and be frightened and sick. He gets cold and hot just like a flu. He has this dream for two months. So they take him to the hospital in the Republic. He goes to the hospital four times, coming back, going again. Every time he has that dream, he has the flu but it's not the flu.

One day an old miner says to Motlatsi, 'My child, this is not a sickness which white people can heal. White people cannot help you because this is our sickness, Basotho sickness. You must go home. When you arrive at home, tell your mother to take you to the Basotho doctor. Maybe he can heal you. If you don't do this, you are going to die in the Republic without seeing your mother again.'

So Motlatsi came home. When he arrived here he told us about the sickness. After that flu there is something moving up and down in his chest. We could look at him and see he was in pain. It blocks his breathing. We see that it throbs under his ribs.

So I took him to the woman *sangoma* in Matsieng. When we were on the way to the *sangoma* I told Motlatsi, 'If this lady asks you, you must say you don't know the name of the man in the dream. If it is a wizard-dream, and this dream is what is making you sick, she can tell you the name of the person who sent the dream. We must be sure who is doing this; I don't want to blame Joseph if it is only something you are making up because you were afraid of him when you were a child. But if the *sangoma* says it is Joseph, we will know. This *sangoma* knows nothing about our family.'

He told the doctor that he started to be sick in the Republic. The doctor says, 'You don't see who is doing this to you, my boy?'

He says, 'No.'

'You don't see the man pulling the small black dog with a green blanket and black trousers and black shoes?'

Motlatsi says, 'No. I do see the man with a horse, but I can't see his face. It's dark there.'

The doctor says, 'You don't see his face?'

Motlatsi says, 'No, I don't know him.'

Doctor says, 'OK, if you don't know him, I don't want to tell you his name. Maybe it's your neighbour. Maybe it's your brother. If I tell you his name, you are going to fight him. My medicine will be spoiled if you do that.'

So I say, "*M'e*, please, I want you to tell us the truth. I won't do anything, and Motlatsi will not fight with this man. It is not my first time to come to you. You have told me everything before, and I didn't fight with anyone; my children didn't fight with anyone. But now this child must know who is doing this to him.'

The lady *sangoma* says, 'OK, I understand. I trust you, *'M'e*. But what I'm going to tell you is bad. This is the uncle of this child. His name is Joseph. When he says "Let's go home, *uena*," to Motlatsi in his dreams, he doesn't mean, "Let's go to your mother's house." I see a small stone house, just built in Roma maybe six months ago; I know that is your house, but that is not where this Joseph wants Motlatsi to go. The uncle doesn't say, "Let's go home to Roma." He wants Motlatsi to go to the mountains where he lived as a child. He wants this young man to go back to work for him as a shepherd, and then he wants to kill him.'

Then she turns to Motlatsi and tells him, 'This man hates your mother because she took her sons away from him. He wanted to use you all like dogs. Because of the medicine this man has, your mother is going to work hard until she dies. The way he has done his medicine, your mother is going to have to pull hard to make her children to grow.'

She says we must not let Joseph know that we know what he is doing. We must not fight with him. He has put this spell on us, and now even if he changes his mind, he doesn't know how to take it away. The *sangoma* says she can't take it all away, but she can help us to protect ourselves. So Motlatsi went back to the mines.

He said he liked working in the mines very much, because he could make some money there. First he worked a year. Then he went back and worked nine months. He came home sick, but he kept working. He had a pain in his side. He had been in a small accident in the mines, had cut off one of his fingers; it was not too bad.

Yet the next time he tried to go to the mines, they refused to take him. Nobody knew why. He paid them two hundred rands to let him go, but still they didn't take him. He didn't think it could be just because he had one finger missing. It was bad luck. So he stayed home and looked for piece-jobs. Sometimes the pain would come in his side, and he would have to go to the hospital for a week, or a few weeks, or sometimes a month. Then he would be better and come home.

Sometimes there was work building houses; more of the time there was nothing for him to do. There has never been work for men in Lesotho, and that is still so. More and more he was sitting at home, drinking *joala*. He said the *joala* helped him to pass the time. He hated sitting home with nothing to do. When he was drunk he used to sing church songs like the Zionists, because he would get the spirit in him to sing. Then he would call Tseliso's children to come and sing with him. He especially liked Ntsoaki. He would sing the whole night, and then suddenly he would say, 'We must sleep before we get angry. Everybody must go to bed. Quick, quick.' He would get angry very quickly sometimes, and he knew when it was coming.

As soon as he started to be angry, he would hit Thuso, Tseliso's oldest girl. He said she was cheeky, and he called her 'big-head girl'. Tseliso would laugh. He never minded if Motlatsi hit his child. So Thuso would come to me, and I would take care of her. I never did think she was cheeky; she just spoke her mind.

In 1986, when the great wind-storm came and blew the roof off my house, Motlatsi was in hospital. But as soon as he could get out of hospital, he came home to help me. He was the one who put the roof back on. He was always the man I could depend on when there was trouble with the house. He was loving me like Tseliso did, although he was very different from Tseliso. He had much anger in him. He would get angry with me, too, and sometimes he would say mean things and then go out of the house. I would never answer back to him, because I knew his anger would go away as quickly as it came.

Motlatsi never slept anywhere but at my house. It was his only home. He never looked for a woman to stay with, because he had no work. He knew he could not pay *lobola*, or bring more children home for me to raise. He respected me enough to know it would drive me mad to have to take care of him and his wife and children too.

So it was exactly a year after Tseliso died, in June of 1988, that Motlatsi began to feel sick. That pain in his side came again, and he got a headache which was so painful he went and just sat on the hill. His feet were swollen twice their normal size. His shoes would not go on. We took him to the hospital, and the first question they asked was, 'Were you ever working in the mines?' That is always the first question they ask a Mosotho man when he arrives at hospital. 'Did you ever be in the mines?' They asked him that every time he went to hospital, and every time he said Yes.

They put him on the TB ward. That was on a Tuesday, and in two days his feet were better. They said it was the cold that made his feet swell. I could not go to see him every day because of my work, but I went on Sunday, and I saw that he was better. He said, 'I am better, *'M'e*,' but he didn't look me in the face. He was looking down at the sheets on the bed. 'I will get better, *'M'e*, so don't worry.'

On Monday I went back to work and sent 'M'athuso to see him. He didn't even talk to her. He just said, 'Oh, my sister, I am sick. Everything is gone.'

'M'athuso was worried. We knew it was Uncle Joseph's medicine again. When she was leaving, Motlatsi said, 'You must come and see me tomorrow early.'

It was only one year since her husband died, and she was feeling much grief. She promised to come and see him, but on the next day, the lady she was working for said she could not go. She said she needed 'M'athuso in the café, and she said she would go to the hospital and come back and tell 'M'athuso how Motlatsi was doing. At two o'clock that lady came back and told 'M'athuso that Motlatsi had passed away.

'M'athuso just sank down on the floor. Her body was so heavy she could not move. She was not fainting. She just could not move, or speak, or do anything for a while. But she knew she had to come tell me. She waited until she knew I would be home from work, and she tried to walk the short distance between the café and my house, but she could not. Her legs would not move. She sank down again on the ground.

A friend of hers saw her and knew what must be wrong. She asked how was Motlatsi in the hospital, and 'M'athuso could not speak. Only her tears began to flow. That friend helped her up, and they walked together to my house. I saw them, and I knew. I stood in my doorway, knowing what they could not say. Motlatsi had passed away, exactly one year after his brother.

Then I did cry, because it was too much. I cried for Motlatsi, and I cried the tears I could not cry for Tseliso, because I was feeling the loss of both of them. Motlatsi never talked very much, except when he drank. He was a quiet man who felt angry sometimes because he could see the trap he was in, with no work and no way to get any work. I knew I could depend on him to help me when I needed help; he was always happy to work for me on the house or to have anything to do that felt useful.

So I had another funeral in June of 1988, a year after the first one. The Burial Society helped me again. Again I took off two weeks from work, for mourning; but the whole month I was troubled. My blood pressure was very high because I was troubled in my heart, thinking how great was my loss of these boys. Joseph came to the funeral, and I saw him looking at Mofihli, and I knew he was going to work on Mofihli next, but there was nothing I could do.

Mofihli started drinking *joala* when he was in his teens. He finished Standard Five and then quit going to school and started drinking. I could not stop him, because I was working all day, and he was not going to school, not working. Maybe he can just work when a person asks him to, sometimes. After that he will take all the money and go drink *joala*.

He could talk nicely. He spoke English well, and he could talk people into giving him piece-jobs. But as soon as he got his pay, he would go drink it all. Tseliso tried to help him, but it was no use. After Tseliso died, there was nobody trying to help Mofihli, and Joseph's medicine had nothing to stop it.

In June 1989, it was very cold. Mofihli got the same thing

Tseliso and Motlatsi had: cold, pain. Pain in the side, pain in the head. We brought him to the hospital. They asked him, 'Did you ever work in the mines?'

He said No.

But they put him on the TB ward anyway. They always say it's TB if they don't know what else to say. They are not going to say this boy has a spell on him. He was there for three weeks. One day I went to visit him, and I saw that he was not going to live. His colour was changed. He didn't look like Mofihli. He said, 'I'm tired. It's better to me to die. These nurses always want to hit me. They think I don't know how to talk English. They tell the *lekoerekoere* doctor that I don't know anything. So I say to the doctor, "You know, Doctor, I know English. My home is Roma, near the University. How can I not know English?"'

He said, 'The *lekoerekoere* doctor said, "Never mind about them. Don't make these nurses angry, because if you talk too much and make them angry, they will give you pills to make you die."' We laughed at that, and it was good to have something to laugh about, because it was not much laughing between us.

He just took only three weeks in hospital and he passed away. It was July 1989. The Burial Society helped with his funeral, and now I have buried three boys in three years. Their graves are close together, at the end of the cemetery close to Christ the King High School. I think maybe Joseph is satisfied. He has taken all those boys who ran away from him in the mountains. Joseph will never go to jail for what he did, but he is already in jail in his mind.

He began to go mad long before my boys were all gone. He would talk to himself; he would be awake all night, or if he slept, he would have bad dreams. The first time his wife took him to the mental hospital in Maseru, Tseliso was still alive. While Joseph was in that hospital, his wife was visiting him, and on the way back home she saw Tseliso in Lithabaneng. She says, '*Lumela*, Tseliso.'

He greeted her.

'How is your mother?'

'Fine.'

'But what does your father want with my husband?'

Tseliso laughs, 'My father?'

'Yes. Your father.'

Tseliso says, 'I was forgetting I ever had a father, because he is long dead.'

She tells him, 'Your father is always after my husband. You know what he has done to Joseph?'

Tseliso says, 'You are talking about dead people. Get out of my way, or I can kick you, because I remember many things about this husband of yours.' And he left her standing there.

After Joseph came out of the hospital, he tried to make a feast to ask for forgiveness from my children, for what he has done to them. But again my children refused to go, just as they refused years before. On the day of this feast, Joseph's child, two months old, suddenly died without being sick. He just stopped breathing. And the people said, 'Yes, it's Alexis. He is angry because of what Joseph is doing with his children.'

The next time Joseph made a feast he didn't even try to get my children to come, but a big cow died on the day of that feast. I don't know whose cow it was; maybe it was Joseph's cow. But the people saw that Joseph was living with bad luck now. And even today this is true. My three sons are dead, and Joseph is alive, but Joseph cannot enjoy his life. He still goes to the mental hospital sometimes, and they give him medicine to help him sleep, but his sleep is not good sleep and it never will be.

CHAPTER 19

Working in Other People's Houses

When I started to work for Mrs Masango, at the University, I left all the children with my mother. Tseliso was sixteen, Manraile eleven, Motlatsi nine, Ralibuseng eight, Mofihli four, and Muso two. None of them knew what was a school, because in Maraka-bei the school was too far away. When they all came together in Roma after Alexis died, I started all of them to school. It was January 1969, and at that time there were no school fees, only ten cents for pencils, so I could send them. They had no uniforms, no shoes, but they all went to Roma Primary School. They were very glad, at first, to go to school. They always saw others going to school, and they were happy to go. Because the people were just learning about what is school, people coming down from the mountains, children would begin Standard One whenever they could do it, and there was no shame from being big. Tseliso was in school with children of all ages in Standard One.

My mother was taking care of the children, and I was making seventeen rand a fortnight, and that is all we had for six children and two adults. It was enough to buy maize meal, paraffin for the stove, soap, and sometimes a few second-hand clothes from the Mission. Everybody had no shoes, so my children were not feeling shame; they only felt the stinging of the stones on their feet, and the ice in winter would make deep cracks in their feet, which would sometimes bleed. I would rub animal fat into those cracks, and they would put their feet close to the fire. It hurt them, but it made the cracks go away.

One of my aunties in Roma was working at the University, cleaning another lady's house, and she told me that somebody arrived who wanted a helper. She told me to go to this new lady and ask for work, but Auntie said I must not say this is my first job. I must say I used to work for another lady who moved away. So I go, I say these things, and Mrs Masongo tells me I can begin to work.

I work for Mrs Masongo, a Mosotho who was married with a Xhosa. On my first day she showed me where her things belonged, and she didn't ask me what I know. She just showed me how she liked it done, and I watched. She wanted me to do washing for her and her husband and their children, ironing, house cleaning. I knew how to do these things, but it was hard for me because it was my first time to work in a big house. The work made me tired, and it was strange to me to have to please another lady all the time, when I was just used to pleasing myself.

I knew how to wash, but I didn't know anything about electricity. I was afraid, maybe I will burn the trousers of Professor Masongo. They had four children, two grown ones in England, and two girls living with them, one in primary school and one in high school. Mrs Masongo taught me how to iron with an electric iron, how to cook meat in an oven, and how to bake cakes and buns. She was nice to me; she spoke Sesotho with me and showed me exactly how to do everything she wanted me to do. At first I work for her from 8 a.m. to 5 p.m.; at five o'clock I go home and find my children at home with my mother. At that time Mrs Masongo did not give me lunch; I had to bring my little bit of *papa* or bread from home. Later, Mrs Masongo moved to a bigger house and gave me a little room at the back, and then I could only see my children on the weekends, but from then I could eat all my meals at Mrs Masongo's house. My room had a narrow bed and a small blue table. I could keep my clothes in a suitcase under the bed and hang a few things on nails on the wall.

Some of my children were proud of their school work; they would show me, and we would talk about it when I came home to be with them. Others did not care so much. Tseliso made friends with some other big boys, and sometimes they did not go to school at all. They would hide in the forest all day and tell us they were in school.

I was just thinking all the time how much I would like to have a house. We were all living in the small rondavel of my mother.

There were holes in the wall and in the thatch of the roof. There was not room on the floor for all of us to sleep; when I sleep I go out to another house, to another lady in front of our house. She was my friend, 'M'ampho. She was the same age as me. She and her two children lived in that house alone because she had no husband, and she let me sleep with her.

One day there was a great wind, and a stone fell from the rondavel and hit my mother on the chest. When my mother was hit, we wanted her to go to the hospital. She said, 'I'm not a child. I'm not sick. I'm not going to the hospital.'

But from that time I was always dreaming to have a house for all of us, not this falling-down rondavel. I would cry to see somebody building a house, even if it's a small house. I would be glad for them, but I would cry because I can't see when I can ever have a house. I was just working for *phofo*. That's what we say when a woman works all the time, as hard as she can, and all she can buy is what she needs to eat, and to feed her children, and maybe even sometimes they can't all eat till the end of the month.

One day I said to my mother, 'I think it's better to me to go home to the mountains to my old house.'

My mother says, 'No, you mustn't go there. God will help you. You can't go to the Maluti because your husband told you he doesn't want you to live there alone. You must stay here so that your children can go to school.'

I say, 'No. I'm going.' I was fed up. Even the work did not make me have hope. I say, 'I have to leave this work with Mrs Masongo and go home to the mountains.' I missed the mountains.

But my mother talked to me, and she prayed, and I could not finally leave her alone in Roma. She was loving the children so much, and me, and she was not even thinking about going to the mountains with me. So I stayed, working in other women's houses.

I started working for Mrs Masongo while Alexis was still in the hospital. When he passed away, the phone call came from the police station to Mrs Masongo's house. She took me with her car to my home in Mafikeng, and she was very kind to me. She knew our custom, that I would have to stay away for a time, and so she told me to find her a person to work in her house while I am away, and I could come back to my job. I say she was kind, because another lady would say if I must leave because my husband is passed away, she would find herself another helper and I have to look for work when my mourning time is over.

When Alexis is buried and I go to the Maluti for two months, I asked 'M'anthabiseng to work for me. 'M'anthabiseng was a good friend to me, but she didn't like working for Mrs Masongo. While I was in the Maluti, 'M'anthabiseng wrote me a letter and told me I should come back to Roma as soon as possible, because she has weak lungs and she doesn't like to work in the house.

So I came back and started my work again. It was good to me to have work, because I needed the money. I liked Mrs Masongo's house. No complaints. Maybe if I had another kind of work I would have liked it better, but this was all I knew.

One day I answered the phone for Mrs Masongo. It was a white man. He said, 'Where is Mrs Masongo? Is she there?'

I call her. After she talks to him she asks me, 'How can this *lekhooa* (white person) talk with you? I thought you said you don't speak English. I thought you could only speak Sesotho, but one day I heard you talking Xhosa, and my children tell me you understand Zulu and speak many languages. I think you are a liar. You say you are a Mosotho from the Maluti Mountains, and you don't know anything. But this is not true.'

I didn't say anything. But she told her children to catch me by talking with me in Xhosa. When I answer them she will know the truth. And this happens. Then another time her sister-in-law comes to visit and speaks Xhosa with me. I answer her, not thinking, and she says, 'Oh, you know how to talk Xhosa!'

She calls Mrs Masongo and says, 'This lady knows how to talk Xhosa and Afrikaans. Be careful around her. She understands everything you say.'

Mrs Masongo says, 'This woman is a *tsotsi*. She told me she didn't understand anything but Sesotho, but she lied.'

And it was partly true. She didn't ask me what languages I speak, and I didn't tell her. I didn't want her to know I understand what she says, no matter what language she speaks. If I walk in and she is saying something bad about me to the children, I understand her words. This is necessary, because when you are working with a person, you can't make her always to be happy with you. You will forget to dust the windowsill one day; you will break a cup, or leave some streaks on the floor from mopping. She will say something about you which she doesn't want you to hear. I pretend I don't understand, but I do, and because of that I can know a little bit what is coming, or why she acts angry when she says nothing to me about what makes her angry.

But after she sets the trap for me with the children and her sister-in-law, we sit down and she asks me, 'Where did you learn this Xhosa?' I tell her I was in Benoni Location, many years in school, and we used to speak Xhosa, Zulu, Sesotho, Afrikaans, Tswana, and Pedi. We would talk English in the classroom, and also at times Afrikaans and Sesotho, or even Xhosa. You never knew from day to day what language you would speak that day. Sometimes when you arrive in the morning the teacher will tell you, 'I don't want any more Xhosa. We will talk only Sesotho today.' Other days he will say, 'We are going to talk Afrikaans the whole day.' And so I told Mrs Masongo that's how I learned these languages. I lived in Benoni ten years; they were the years of my schooling, though I didn't go to school every year the whole time.

After this, Mrs Masongo was careful when she talked about me. She would go behind a closed door, or whisper, 'Sh! The maid will hear you.'

Mrs Masongo is dead now, but she would be even more surprised to know the maid is writing a book about everything that happened.

I remember the first time I got money for the work I did, I was very very glad, because I knew my children were going to eat, and I even bought some sugar for the house. It felt different than when Alexis gave me money, because my pay was seventeen rands; when Alexis gave me money it was thirty pounds. That was a lot of money in the mountains; I could buy anything I like with it. My little money in Roma was not for much besides *phofo*, but I was happy to get it, because for several years I had no money at all. When I began to live in Mrs Masongo's house, she cut my pay from seventeen rands a fortnight to twenty-two rands a month, and I continued at that pay for eight years, until 1977, when we had the problem with the earrings.

In 1977 Mrs Masongo went to London for a holiday, to stay six months. Her grown daughter was working there, and she was going to stay with her. She left me with *Ntate* Masongo and the two girls, and she said, 'Be sure you don't ever let anyone in my bedroom except *Ntate*.'

I didn't think anything about this, and we went on living as we always did, no troubles, until *Ntate* brought home a lady he was going to sleep with while his wife was away.

One morning *Ntate* Masongo went to town and bought a fried chicken. He told me that at nine o'clock at night, I should put the chicken in the oven to be warm. He said a lady was coming with *papa*, and I just needed to cook spinach. The lady was a nurse, working in the hospital; that's why dinner was going to be so late. He brought her into the kitchen and introduced her to me when she arrived. I didn't want to meet her, but what could I do? I greeted her nicely, and they passed to the sitting room. *Ntate* said, 'You can go and sleep, 'M'atsepo. It's not your time to be in the kitchen now. I will wash the dishes.'

So I go to my room and sleep. The next day she was gone before I got up, and from then on she always came late at night and left early. I did not have to speak to her again. But I knew she was sleeping in Mrs Masongo's bedroom, and I remembered Mrs Masongo told me not to let anyone in her bedroom except *Ntate*. But it was his house. I could not tell him not to take the lady in there.

When Mrs Masongo came home, a friend of hers told her about the lady who was sleeping with Mr Masongo while she was away, and she told Mrs Masongo that I was a *tsotsi* because I let this lady stay there with him. She seemed to think I could stop *Ntate* from doing what he liked in his bedroom when his wife was gone. It was his house. I am a maid. I don't know anything.

Two weeks after Mrs Masongo came back from London she said a pair of her earrings are lost. I ask her, 'What kind of earrings are they?'

She told me.

I said, 'I don't know anything about them. I think I never saw any earrings like those.'

She says, 'That means that when I was not here, you let somebody come in my house, look in my wardrobe, and take my things.'

I say, 'No, *'M'e*. I never touched the wardrobe since you went away. Even when I washed the clothes of *Ntate* Masongo, I put them on the bed. He takes them and puts them on a hanger in the wardrobe. So I don't know anything about these earrings.' I didn't want to say anything about whether somebody came into her bedroom. What could I say? It was not my business to tell her what her husband was doing.

She was angry. On Friday she told me that I must stay at home for two weeks with no pay and think about those earrings. She said, 'This is a holiday I am giving you for two weeks. You think about those earrings and come back on Monday, two weeks from now.'

I finish my holiday and go back to work on Sunday night, like I used to when I spent the weekend at home, but there was nobody in the house. I had to walk back home in the dark. So on the next morning, Monday, I come very early. I find Mrs Masongo's daughter in the kitchen. I greet her and ask her, 'Where were you last night?'

She says, 'We were in Maseru. We came back late, at midnight.'

'Why didn't you leave the key for me?'

She says, 'I don't know, *'M'e*. I don't know what is going on.' The child looked very serious and sad. I could see something was wrong. She was preparing her food for going to school. I tried to prepare the food for breakfast for *Ntate* and Mrs Masongo, but Mrs Masongo comes in the kitchen and finds me.

'*Lumela*, 'M'atsepo,' she greet me in a big voice, looking very angry.

I answer, '*Lumela*, *'M'e*.'

She didn't ask how I am. She just passed through the kitchen and went out. Then *Ntate* came and greeted me, asked how are my children these two weeks.

I answered him, 'They are well.' I gave him food. He ate, and he went to work. Mrs Masongo went out without eating. I thought she was going to her office to work, but in a short time she came back. She called one of the gardeners, *Ntate* Lepota, and she said, 'Come here, *'M'e* 'M'atsepo, to my room.'

I go, and she says, *'Ntate* Lepota, sit down here with us.' We all sit, wondering what is happening. She says, *'Ntate* Lepota, I'm sorry, because I have to send 'M'atsepo away. We have worked together for eight years, but today I have to let her go and rest. I think she is tired. So I want you to be the witness. I lost my earrings. I don't say she is stealing.'

Ntate says, 'Maybe the children have taken the earrings.'

She says, 'I can't chase my children away.'

Ntate says, 'Is it because of the earrings, or are you tired of working with *'M'e* 'M'atsepo?'

She says, 'I'm not tired, but I see that she is tired.'

I say, 'Thanks, *'M'e*, for working with me so nicely. If you are tired of working with me, I understand.'

'I'm not tired. You are tired.' And her voice is very hard.

I say, 'Thanks, *'M'e*, God bless you.' And I never go to the kitchen again from that time. I go to my room and begin to pack my things.

She says, 'When you are ready, tell me. I can take you home with my car.'

I say, 'Yes,' but I don't do that. I take my time with my packing. I pack, I sit on the bed and remember many things from those eight years. I was going to say good-bye to her children, who were just like my own. I packed again. At four o'clock, when the people who were working in the offices and the houses started to go home, I asked another lady to help me with my things. When we were taking my things out the back door I saw Mrs Masongo, and I said, *'Sala hantle, 'M'e*, stay well.'

She looked ashamed, but I was not angry. I was *'M'e* 'M'atsepo, who never changed.

When I arrived at home, I told my mother what happened. She said, 'You and Mrs Masongo – there must be something which is happening between the two of you. You are not people who will do this. There must be bad luck on one of you.'

But I didn't tell my mother about the nurse who came to sleep with *Ntate* Masongo. I stayed at home for two weeks. After that I found a job again, in Maseru, with Mrs Mohapi. I got this job because a good friend of Mrs Masongo found me one day at the bus stop and said, "*M'e* 'M'atsepo, I don't want you to stay at home with no work. I don't know what makes you to have trouble with '*M'e* Masongo. She is my friend, but I don't understand this. This doesn't feel right to me. You are a person who always works nicely. You don't talk. When she shouts at you, you don't talk back. So I don't know what happened. But I know of a lady in Maseru. She is cruel, but I think you can work for her. Let's go to Maseru, and I will show you where her house is.'

So we went there. She introduced me to Mrs Mohapi. She seemed to be a nice lady, but her heart was not nice. I worked there for three months, but it seemed like three years. Every day I was tense; I got a headache.

At the beginning, the first two days, everything was OK. After that she said, 'Shame! You were working for Mrs Masongo eight years?'

I said, 'Yes.'

'I can't work with you. I can't believe it.'

I didn't ask why.

'You don't know how to iron. You don't know how to cook. So I don't know what were you doing those eight years.'

At that same time Mrs Masongo moved to Maseru, and her children came to see me and showed me their new house. They said, 'We think our mother was wrong to fire you.'

But I heard Mrs Mohapi go ask Mrs Masongo, 'How did you work with '*M'e* 'M'atsepo?'

Mrs Masongo says, 'She was a good lady. We worked nicely together. I can't tell you what happened at the end, but she is good.'

Later Mrs Masongo tells me, "*M'e* 'M'atsepo, I know this lady. She is cruel. She comes from Johannesburg. You can never please her. She can't ever say anything nice.'

But Mr Mohapi was very good. He would try to make his wife treat me like a human being. I was eating bread and tea for breakfast, bread and tea for lunch, bread and tea at night. So one day Mr Mohapi asked his wife, 'What is this '*M'e* eating?'

'Bread and tea.'

'From morning till night?'

'Yes. What can I do? I told her there is cabbage in the garden, if she wants to eat something besides bread and tea.'

Mr Mohapi says, 'What are you eating? Bread and tea?'

She says, 'No. This is my house. I eat what I like.'

But he says, 'Bread and tea from morning till night can make a person sick. If she gets sick from staying with you, it's not good, really.' He began to be angry, and he said, 'That's why your helpers are always leaving you. You starve them and complain just like a Boer woman. You are cruel. You don't like people. You don't care how they live.'

She was paying me twenty-four rands a month, plus a room to sleep in, and this bread and tea. When I got my money I would bring it to Roma and keep a little bit and buy a little meat, just once a month. Sometimes Mr Mohapi would come into the kitchen and put a little money into my hand secretly. He said I must not tell his wife. But Mr Mohapi was not staying at home for long. He would always go to other countries, travelling to Zambia, America, England. He only stayed at home a few days at a time, because he was a diplomat in the government of Leabua Jonathan. Mrs Mohapi was not working, just staying at home all day, watching me while I work.

One day at Mrs Mohapi's house was like this: a little before 7 a.m. I wake up. I wash myself in the little bathroom and I go to the kitchen. I knock at the door, and Mrs Mohapi opens it. We greet each other, and she complains, 'It is five past seven. You are only now waking up?'

I say, 'It's seven.'

She says, 'You're mad. You sleep like a dead thing, as if you are in your own house.'

I don't answer. I just pass her and take my broom and start to clean the veranda. She follows me. I am kneeling down, taking a cloth to wipe the veranda. She says, 'What are you doing? You are trying to cheat me. You think you are cleaning this veranda? I have cleaned it myself. I have been up a long time. I don't sleep like you. I have finished cleaning the veranda and I want my house to be clean. I have a party at seven o'clock this evening.'

The house was always clean. You can't even find a speck of dirt the size of a fingernail. The rug was green like grass, and anything that falls on this rug shows. There is never anything there. But I go in and clean the house where it is already clean. Sometimes I just go up and down and clean the clean floors so she sees I am busy.

But that day I was working hard to prepare for supper at 7 p.m. for many people. Mr Mohapi was arriving home from overseas. The soldiers of Leabua Jonathan were there, and twelve more diplomats were coming, and the King was coming too. I saw them when they arrived. Some of them brought their wives, but the Queen did not come. Mrs Mohapi served them, and then she ate with them. They had very beautiful clothes; I could see when the kitchen door opened. But I did not serve them. I stayed in the kitchen all day and all night, working, with no food. I had to do everything before I could eat, and I worked till 2 a.m.

The dishes were coming in and going out. I was the only one in the kitchen. Mrs Mohapi did all the cooking, and I was smelling that food all day but could not eat anything. By seven o'clock I was very hungry. The hours pass: 9, 10, 11, 12. By 1 a.m. I was so hungry I took some salad that was left on a plate. It had mayonnaise, and it was warm, and it poisoned me. By three or four o'clock I was vomiting, stomach aching, diarrhoea. But it was no use, because at seven o'clock the next morning I must be knocking at the kitchen door. I was tired, and Mrs Mohapi greeted me,

'You are always late!'

I said I was not feeling very well.

'Oh well,' she says, 'So what?'

I look at her and think it's a pity. I think, 'When I go from here, she won't see me any more.' Out loud I tell her I have to go home for my daughter's wedding. It was not true; Manraile was married in 1975. But I say I am going, and I will come back after the wedding.

Mr Mohapi comes for his breakfast, and he hears me talking. He asks me, 'Are you coming back, *'M'e*?'

I say, 'Yes, I will come back. After the wedding.'

When I was packing my things, Mrs Mohapi comes into my room and says, 'She is taking everything. She will not come back.' Her husband looks sad, but he doesn't say anything.

I packed everything that was mine. I washed my overall dresses which belonged to Mrs Mohapi, and I left them on the bed, washed and folded nicely. Then Mr Mohapi takes me with his car to the bus stop. He asks again, 'Are you coming back, *'M'e*? I know my wife. People always do this. I told her she will never find a person to work for her who is as good as you.'

I say, 'No, *Ntate*, I will come back. Don't worry.' But in my heart I know I am not coming back. I couldn't tell him the truth because I felt sorry for him. I didn't want him to be angry with his wife. It was the last time I ever saw him.

For a long time I was without regular work. I did what I could, a few days work here and there. Then in 1978 and '79 I worked for a young white man who was a lecturer. Mrs Masongo recommended me to work for him, and I worked for him just three days a week. He paid me thirty rands a month and was very nice to work for. I washed, ironed, cleaned the house. He didn't stay at home much, but sometimes the students came to his house for a lecture, and then there would be a lot of cleaning up afterwards. He was in education. He was only here one year and then he had to go to Botswana, so I was looking for work again.

My mother started to be sick in October 1979. We could all see that she was not well, but she pushed herself, trying to do her things as always. She was weak, and she started to have a pain in her chest. She went to the clinic and got some pills, which made her a little bit better, but after two weeks she started to cough. Then her knees were not strong enough to hold her. If she wanted to walk, she had walk around the edges of the house, so she could hold onto the wall. I wondered what it was, and I took her to the clinic. There a doctor gave her some cough mixture, which helped for a little while.

She told me, 'My child, I don't like you to go to work in Maseru and leave the children here alone. I'm going to pray for God to help you find a good job so you can stay at home.' She said she would help me, even if she died.

She passed away on January 20 1980. My cousin bought a coffin for her. I just bought one sheep with my little money. My mother always said she wanted to die before me so I could bury her properly, with a priest, and I made sure that she had a proper funeral. I was very sad; there was never anyone in my life I loved more than my mother. But because she was sick, I thought it was better for her to rest. She always loved God, and I knew she would feel at home with Him. I also knew she would never leave me; that she would stay with me and help me whether she was alive or not. That is still true.

Soon after my mother died, the woman who was working in the guest house was fired from her job for stealing, so then the guest house had no cleaning person. The man I last worked for, the one who went to Botswana, told his friends to look out for a job for me, and with my mother's help, in August 1980, I started to work in the guest house and I am working there until now. The guests are coming in and going out, changing every day.

I do their washing, ironing, and cleaning. I keep everything like a hotel: I keep a count of the dishes and replace them if they break; I buy tea, sugar, soap, toilet paper. Sometimes there are many guests; I can have four in one part of the house and a family, maybe five or six people, in the other part. But even when there are no guests, I work and keep the house and the garden so that when people come they find the house a nice place to stay.

In the beginning I had many troubles with this job. Sometimes I would spend two or three months without pay. When I go and ask for my money they treat me like a fool. They say they need a letter from the Domestic Bursar. When I go to the Domestic Bursar they tell me they need a letter from somewhere else. When I go to that office they tell me to go back to the first office I went to and get a stamp. I go there and they tell me, 'What stamp? There is no stamp here.'

In the beginning, when they paid me at all, they paid me sixteen rands for two weeks, which was not enough even for *phofo*, because the cost of food was going up so fast. So I prayed to my mother, 'Mother, you gave this job to me. Please take these troubles away.' And she did.

Now nothing worries me except when my money is finished

before the end of the month and I have no food for my grand-children. Now I make more money; I make three hundred thirty rands a month. But all the prices have gone up, so much that I cannot keep enough food in the house from one pay day to the next.

Sometimes the people who come to the guest house are very special; I like to talk with them and learn about where they come from. I like to know everything I can. Once a man and his wife came from England, and they asked me to make a tape of Sesotho for them to study; they gave me an English dictionary for a gift when they left. Many Africans from other countries come; we call them *makoerekoere* because we cannot understand their talking and we say it sounds like they are saying, '*Koere koere koere koere.*'

Another time there was one man who came from Holland. He lived one month in the guest house, waiting for his wife to come, but his wife could not come, so he went back to Holland. While he was in the guest house I helped him to learn a little Sesotho, and every Friday he gave me ten rands to buy food for the children. He asked me many questions about the children. At that time it was before my sons died; I told him my children were big but not working. They came home from the mines but were sitting at home, not finding work.

He always said he was missing his wife and his two children, so much that he felt he could not stay here without them. He didn't tell the University he was going. He just told me, and I felt very sorry to see him go. I thought that was the last time I would ever hear of him, but he surprised me.

In 1986 a terrible windstorm came in October and blew the roof off my house. I was losing everything – the only photo I had of my mother, all my important papers, everything blew away, and some of us were hurt when things fell on us. We were so afraid. I don't know how to tell what it is like when the whole roof blows off your house and the rain comes and everything you have is blowing away or being ruined.

This Dutchman must have been writing letters with some other people at the University, because he heard what happened to me – that the whole of my roof was gone, all my things were ruined, and we were having to sleep in the houses of other people. So the Dutchman sent to a friend of his at the University a cheque from Holland, and he told this man to give me seven hundred rands to get help to put the old roof back on the house. Then I was able to fix the roof and buy some food, too. I didn't know his address, to thank him, but I thanked him in my heart, and I think he knew. Maybe he will find this book and read it.

CHAPTER **20**

Sephefu's Two Wives

When I was eight years old and my mother took me first to Roma and then to Benoni, we left my brother, Sephefu, in Mokhokhong with my grandmother. He was thirteen, then, and *Nkhono* wanted him with her. The next time I saw him was two years later. He was working in the mines in Gauteng, and he arrived in Benoni with another miner who knew my father.

That miner said, 'I came with this boy. He told me that he's your child.'

My father was very glad to see him, because he left him long ago. He says to Sephefu, 'I want you to come and stay with us, here in the Location. I don't want you to work in the mines.'

My brother didn't say Yes or No. He didn't know what work he could find in Benoni. At the end of the month my father went to the mine where Sephefu was working and brought him home to Benoni and took him to a factory there, where he could work, making clothes and blankets. My father knew many people at the factory because he once worked there himself, so he found Sephefu a job without any trouble.

Sephefu stayed with *'M'e* and *Ntate* and me. In the morning he would go to work with my mother, because she was working in that same factory, sewing sacks for pieces of wood; I would go to school. We were not staying together a long time, because soon after Sephefu found a wife and brought her home, I went to be married with Alexis.

When Alexis and I moved to the Maluti, for a long time I knew nothing about what happened to Sephefu and his wife. My parents moved to Roma and left Sephefu in the house in Benoni. I was having children in the Maluti; he and his wife were having children in Benoni. Later I found out he moved back to Mokhokhong, where we lived together as children, because that's where Sephefu was killed, in a fight over a woman.

This wife of Sephefu's, 'M'athato, was always running away from him. One time she took their three children and went home to Leribe, to stay with her mother. So Sephefu found another wife, a young woman with a small child. But 'M'athato came back when she heard that Sephefu had got another woman. She came and asked my mother to tell her son that she was back. She wanted to see him and to give her excuses for leaving him, to say she is sorry and she wants to come home.

So my mother goes to Mokhokhong and tells my brother to come to Mafikeng to see his first wife so they could talk together. My brother comes and says to 'M'athato, 'Where do you come from?

She says, 'From Leribe.'

'Who asked you to come again? Are you tired?'

She says, 'Yes. I'm tired because of your father, *Ntate* Lillane, who is dead. First he was troubling the children.' And she tells what happened with the children. 'The children say they were staying in the fields near Leribe, where they were shepherds living in a little hut in the mountains. One day they see a man with one leg. He takes them by their hands, and he says, "Come, let's go to Mokhokhong."'

And they go with him. So one of the herdboys who was working with them, he sees them walking away; but this boy doesn't see the man with one leg. Only my brother's two boys see the man.

The herdboy calls to Sephefu's sons, he says, 'Where are you going?'

They say, 'We are going with this *Ntate* with only one leg. He says we must follow him to Mokhokhong.'

So this herdboy runs home and tells the brother of 'M'athato. He says, 'Those two boys from Mokhokhong, they say they are going home with a man who has one leg. But there is no man. What can this mean?'

So the uncle took his horse and went to find them on the way. He hit them like they were dogs, asking them, 'Where are you going? How can you leave my sheep in the hills and no one to watch them?'

They can't answer. They find no words in their mouths to speak.

So they do this three times. After these three times this man with one leg goes to their mother. He arrives by dream and tells 'M'athato, 'I don't want my children to be watching sheep in the hills of Leribe. I want them in Mokhokhong.'

The first time she didn't take care. She thought it was a dream only.

The second time it came, she woke up and she was sick, very sick. When the people ask her, 'What's matter with this sickness?' she says, 'I can't even talk. I don't know how to explain. The voice which was at night, it was horrible to me. I see that it's better to me to go home to Mokhokhong.'

So the next day when she wakes up, she just says to these children, 'Let's go.' She takes the children and goes by foot from Leribe to the Roma Valley, to Mokhokhong. She was thin, wearing rags of blankets. Even the children were poor, walking by foot from Leribe. No shoes, no trousers.

So my brother listens to this story about our father and the boys and the dream, and he says, 'It's OK. You can come home. You will find your house and sit down. I've got a wife, so if you remain as my wife too, you'll be one of two wives. You won't remain in the same house. You will each have a house.'

She says, 'OK, I'm not going today. I'll go tomorrow. I'm still washing my clothes.'

But the children go with their father to Mokhokhong the same day.

So 'M'athato is left with my mother. She washes her rags, blankets. My mother gave her a little dress; she wore it and went to Mokhokhong, so there are two wives of one man there.

So one day there came a man to Sephefu. He said, 'I want my wife.' He wanted the second one, 'M'alerato.

Sephefu says 'I've got no wife of yours. We must go to the Chief about that wife you need. This is my wife. I have paid *lobola* for both of my wives.' And it was true.

So they go to the Chief. The Chief told that man, ''M'alerato is Sephefu's wife. I have seen the cows and I have written here, *lobola* paid by Sephefu Lillane for this lady. So I don't know how you can say she's your wife.'

The man says, 'It's my wife because I made her pregnant. I went to work in Gauteng, then I came back and I found she is with Sephefu, and he takes my child also.'

Maybe it was true that this man made 'M'alerato pregnant before Sephefu took her to be his wife, but this man also had another wife and children somewhere in the mountains. It was not only Sephefu taking two wives. And it was also true that this man never paid *lobola* for the woman he made pregnant. So the Chief says, 'You must come with your parents and we must see whose wife is this.'

The man says, 'No, I won't come with my parents. I know what I shall do.'

And he goes away. Nobody knows what he will do, or when he will come back.

One day he came again. He went to the Chief and said to the Chief, 'Call Sephefu from the fields.'

A man was sent for Sephefu, and he told Sephefu that the man who claimed to be 'M'alerato's husband was back, waiting for him at the Chief's house.

Sephefu came to the Chief's house with his *molamu*; he found that many people were in the house, waiting for him when he arrived. Sephefu came in angry. When he just walked into the house, the man was suddenly afraid. The man took out his gun and shot four times. Four bullets. The first three missed. Sephefu came toward the man with his *molamu* raised, to beat the man. The last bullet went through Sephefu's eye and out the back of his head.

The Chief says, 'Catch this man!'

And the men were stupid. They caught Sephefu, who was dead, but they let the man with the gun run away. They said no one could catch him.

So they have to go to the police station and tell the police that someone has killed a man at the Chief's house, and the man who killed Sephefu was arrested. When the police talked to him, he said he was not planning to kill Sephefu that day; he was going to talk about this problem with the wives. But when Sephefu came through the door with his *molamu*, he was scared and he killed Sephefu in front of everybody, because everybody can see that if he did not shoot the gun, Sephefu would kill him.

They put him in the jail, but he was missed from the jail. He escaped. When the police found him in his house, in the mountains, they took him back to jail. Again he ran away from the jail. He was wanted the whole year; they didn't find him. After a long time I think they stopped looking for him. He never came back for Sephefu's second wife.

Even now, 'M'athato and 'M'alerato, the two widows of Sephefu, are still in Mokhokhong. I like both of them, but 'M'alerato doesn't like me. Now 'M'alerato is studying to be a *sangoma*. She was my favourite, and I loved her children like my own. After Sephefu died they would come to visit me; they called me their father because I was his sister, and I was very close to those children. But she said her children liked me too much, so she got jealous. She didn't want them to call me their father. So I leave it alone. I have enough children to feed and dress and send to school anyway.

CHAPTER 21

’M’e ’M’ampho and the Snake

Around 1982, ’M’e ’M’ampho’s sister called me to come to see her. ’M’e ’M’ampho was my closest friend; she is the lady I slept with before I had my own house, when there was not room for me to sleep with all my children in my mother’s rondavel. So when I came to her, ’M’e ’M’ampho showed me her ribs on the right side and said, ‘I’m sore here. What’s happening?’

It was green, and there were two marks, red and bloody. I said it must be a spider that bit her. I helped her as much as I could and left her with her younger sister, because I had to go back to work.

After two days ’M’e ’M’ampho came to be very sick. Her bed was too hot, so she put a mat on the floor and waited there till four o’clock, when people would be coming home from work.

When I came back, her sister said, ‘’M’e ’M’atsepo, help me to put ’Me ’M’ampho back on her bed, because now it’s late.’

So when she was trying to make the bed fresh, she smoothed it evenly and she saw something under the bedspread. She said, ‘’M’e ’M’atsepo, come and help me!’ and we thought it was a mouse in the bed. When we tried to catch it, we found a snake, and we saw it go under the bed. ’M’e ’M’ampho saw everything, but she was sick and couldn’t help us.

So we took the bed apart, one piece at a time, and took it all outside. We saw a hole next to the wall by the bed. So we filled the hole with sand. When we finished doing that, we saw one plank of wood on the ground, a small plank about a foot long, and when we picked it up, we saw the snake.

The snake was the length of my elbow to the tips of my fingers, and as thick as two fingers. Its head was small, like the top of a worm. In Sesotho we call it *masumu*. I chased the snake with

'M'e 'M'ampho's sister, but it disappeared again. We kept search-
ing until we found it, and then she took a hoe and chopped it into
three pieces. I could not do that myself, because I was too much
afraid of the snake. After the snake was dead, *'M'e* 'M'ampho's
brother came in and took the three pieces of the snake and put
them in the fire. By then it was dark and all the bed was lying on
the ground outside the house.

One lady came and told us to take these three burned pieces of
snake, put them in a bottle of cold water, and put in a little bit of
salt. If it was a snake of God, she said, it would stay black; if it
was a wizard's snake, it would once again have the colours it had
before it was burned. So we put it in the water and we went to
sleep on mats on the floor.

Next morning the snake was yellow with black spots again,
just like before we burned it, so we knew it was a wizard's snake.
We left it in the bottle. That afternoon the lady came back and
asked us, 'Why do you sit with this thing?'

We tell her, 'We don't know what to do.'

'Go and find the *sangoma* who lives at Popanyane,' she told us.

So we leave the snake in the bottle and go that same day on
foot, and find a lady *sangoma* who told us, before we told her
anything, 'You have come here to ask what happened to a lady
who is sick. She was bitten by a snake, and that snake was sent
to go and bite her, to make her die. The people who sent the
snake were jealous because she has a house and bed and a few
little things which she got by working for other ladies. They don't
want her to have anything. They think she must remain poor
until she dies.'

So the *sangoma* gave us a little bit of medicine to give *'M'e*
'M'ampho when we arrive home. We just pay only two rands, and
we go back home and tell *'M'e* 'M'ampho what this doctor says.
But *'M'e* 'M'ampho was very sick, and the medicine from the
sangoma didn't help her.

In the morning we have to take *'M'e* 'M'ampho to the hospital.
We go with the snake in the bottle to the hospital, so the doctor
can see the snake and know how to treat *'M'e* 'M'ampho. By now
it is six days since the snake bit her. She had to sleep in the
hospital for a week and get treatment for the snakebite. She got

better at the end of a week, and the hospital sent her home. She walked from the post office till she arrived at home, by foot. She was better.

But next morning she was very, very sick again. She could not even walk. The next day we wake up very early and put her in the wheelbarrow to the bus stop to take her to her home in Mafeteng. We think maybe there is a doctor at her home who can help her. I go with her to the bus stop and leave her sister to go with her to Mafeteng, because I have to go to work.

'M'e 'M'ampho stayed in Mafeteng the whole year. One day after she was gone a few months, I went to visit her and found she was very much better. She told me that she missed her house, but she was afraid to go home again, because maybe another wizard-snake will come. I told her we were missing her, but we know she must stay in Mafeteng until she is better.

All while she was gone I was sleeping in her house with her sister, but I was not afraid, because I knew it was not a true snake. It was a wizard-snake, and it was only after 'M'e 'M'ampho, not me. Finally after the whole year had passed she came back to her home. She was all well, and no more snakes. Nothing bad. She is still living in that house now.

CHAPTER 22

Sangomas

Since I was a little girl I have gone to *sangomas* for sickness which is not of God. We call this sickness 'wizard' sickness, or 'spells'. Such sickness needs Basotho medicine, traditional medicine. It cannot be helped by doctors in hospitals or clinics.

I think the first time I met a *sangoma* was when I was fourteen or sixteen, in Benoni. One day when I was in school I just wanted to cry. I didn't know why. When I arrived home, my auntie was there. She said, 'Can I give you bread with tea?'

I say, 'No. I just feel fed up. I don't know why.'

She asks me, 'Are you sick?' and I begin to cry. Just cry and cry, can't stop.

She calls my father. He was in the next yard. He asks, 'Mpho, why are you crying?'

I can't answer him, just keep on crying.

He says, 'I will have to beat her! Why is she crying?'

My auntie says, 'No, don't beat her. Maybe she's sick.'

She takes snuff and puts it in my nose. I sneeze. But I am still crying, can't stop. After that my auntie is worried. She says to my father, 'Let me talk to this girl.' Then she asks me, 'Are you sick?'

I say, 'No, my heart just wants to cry. I want to go home.'

'Which home? You are at home.'

'Lesotho. I'm tired of Benoni,' and I cry again. Cry and cry.

My father is watching. He says there is an Indian doctor in Tenth Street. We go. It was late in the afternoon. We enter there and sit down. The Indian lady doctor comes. She takes a clean tissue and tells me to breathe, 'Haaaa' on it.

I breathe on it. 'Haaa'.

She takes a clean saucer and puts water in it and puts the

tissue in the saucer. And in that paper I saw a short man with a cap and with a stick. He was the ugliest thing I ever saw in my life. It was a *thokolosi*, a bad spirit.

She says, 'This is sent by a boy who wants to marry you. You had a boyfriend who wanted to marry you, and you said "Yes". Later on, you told him you don't love him because your mother doesn't like him. You know if your mother doesn't like him, you must say "No".

'But the man was angry, so he went to a witchdoctor and asked for a *thokolosi* to make you mad. He makes you cry to go back to Lesotho, because the boy who loves you lives in Vereeniging, a place which looks like the Roma Valley of Lesotho, and he wants you to come to him. He says if you don't come to him, this *thokolosi* will make you go mad and run up and down, tearing off your clothes.'

My father asks me, 'Do you know this boy?'

I say, 'Yes, I know him. He's the long, tall boy who was staying at Eighth Street.'

So my father looks at the Indian doctor and says, 'Please, help my child not to go mad.'

The doctor gave me medicine to wash my body and told me to talk to this boy and tell him to leave me alone. And I got better. I went to school again, and it was no more crying.

The second time I had such a sickness was when I was seventeen years old. I come from school. The lady next door calls to me. She asks me, 'Mpho, come and open the door for me. Maybe this key is refusing to work because it's not my key; maybe because this is your father's house, you can open it.'

I go. I touch the key. It was in the door. I put my hand on it, but before I try to open the door, she says 'No, leave it, I see what the problem is. I didn't have it in the keyhole the right way. I see that you don't know any better than me.'

She just takes the key and opens the door at the same time.

I think nothing of all this. I go home, I go to sleep. I wake up and go to scool. The next day when I was in school, I was playing with a big ball and I jammed my thumb just a little bit. When I entered in the school after playing, my right hand was shaking. When I just took a pencil and tried to write, my hand jerked and went off the page. I tried to get control of it by taking my left hand and guiding it, but it refused. The teacher asked, 'What's wrong with your hand?'

I say, 'I don't know.'

'Is it hurt?'

I say, 'I don't know. It' s just sore.'

He says it's no use staying in school if I can't use my right hand – I should just go home and let my parents see what is happening. He says maybe I hurt it playing ball. I should go home.

And I go home. I tell my father. He sees the hand. He tries to bandage it to be still, but now the hand was sore. In the morning when we wake up the hand was green. It was all green from the wrist to the elbow. He takes me to the clinic, and the doctor says,

'This is a poison. We can't help it.' But they give us medicine for rubbing. And we go home.

After we arrive, maybe seven or eight at night, my father says, 'No, I can't sleep with this person. They tell me this is a poison, so I can't sleep with a poisoned person.'

We go to that Indian doctor again. When I arrive the Indian doctor says, 'Oh, you are here again, Mpho. You will finish the money of this good old man, your father.'

She gave me four cards, just regular playing cards, four of them, and said I must rub them between my hands. I rub them and I put them down, and the doctor takes these cards and looks at them. She says, 'Oh, I see. The lady who lives next door to you calls you and says you must open her door with a key. The lady put something on the key so that when you just touch it, this hand will be poisoned, and if the soreness goes up your arm to your heart, you can die.'

We ask, 'Why did she do this?'

'The lady is jealous. She says, "Why doesn't Mpho get pregnant, like our children?" She thinks you are acting like you are better than her children, so she is going to kill you. She sees you are always sitting at home in the yard, never going out with other children, as if you think you are better.'

So the doctor gave me the medicine again and she cuts many little cuts with a razor, all the way up my arm. The cuts are bleeding, and after the blood comes out, she takes the medicine and puts it in the cuts so it can enter and stop the poison before it gets to my heart. And she tells my father, 'I'm going to help you, because I see this lady wants to kill your child. Is twice this child has been here, so I am going to take this poison and send it back to the lady who tried to kill Mpho.'

And she gives us medicine and says she is speaking to that lady, saying, 'This poison must go back to you again!'

So the next day we see it worked. The lady was like me. The whole of her right arm and her right leg are paralyzed. The lady comes to my father and says, 'Oh *Ntate* Johannes, I didn't know I would be like this. Somebody has made me to be like this.'

My father says, 'You started it. So you must see now how nice is it when you are like that.'

She says, 'I am sorry for what I have done.'

But she was paralyzed on the right side until she died.

The third sickness was the lady in the other yard next door. I was maybe eighteen. I had something in my chest going up and down, up and down, even when I swallow. I try to drink water. When I drink, the water goes down and it comes back up. It was very painful. I take two days with this. I didn't know what is happening. I thought is tonsils, because tonsils is my sickness. From there I told my father, 'Oh there is something here, in my chest, moving up and down. I am not eating. Don't want even to eat, because when I eat, the food starts to come back up.' So I was not eating for two days.

My father took me again to that lady, *Lekula*, the Indian doctor. When I arrived there the Indian says, 'Ow! This child! You want to finish the money of the old man. You are always coming here with your troubles. This is no good, my dear. These people are trying to kill you. And I am going to kill them too. I am tired of them. I am going to make the thing in you to go to the owner. So say now, what's the matter?'

I say something is going up and down, up and down inside me.

She says, 'OK, sit down. I will help you.'

She calls her son. This son was called Boya, we called him Boy. She says, 'Come and help me. Take the mug and bring me some water.'

And he takes the water and puts some medicine in the water,

like a teaspoonful. And she says I must drink this medicine. I drink it. After that she says to take a wash basin and go outside and vomit. I go with that boy. I vomit. And the thing comes out. I didn't see that there is something which falls in the basin, but when I finish, the boy takes the basin with the vomit in it and takes a Sesotho broom and pours the water over it so it is like a sieve. And the thing from the vomit comes on the broom. It was small, like a pellet from a sheep.

And the doctor says to bring it to her. The boy gives it to his mother, and the mother takes a knife and cuts it. In it we find hair. The doctor says, 'They are trying to make you mad again. But it's not going to work. I am going to help you again and again, and when these people see you, they will be ashamed for what they have done. When they see you coming this way, they will look away, or they will cross the street. They can't face you.'

So she gave us medicine again for that thing which I have vomited. She says I must run and buy a small Vaseline. I go. She says, 'I am tired of these people.'

I come with the small Vaseline. She puts the medicine in the small Vaseline, and she says, 'You must use it, put it on your face before you go anywhere, and you will be all right.' And I was better.

That's why I like the Basotho doctors or the *sangomas*, because I always – as we say – 'grow hard.' Strong. From experience. I learn from these things. I live through these things, and I learn from them. I like the traditional doctors because I know they can make me well when I have a sickness which is not from God. I have seen it.

Sometimes you go to a *sangoma* who is not good. Sometimes they tell you something you don't understand. They are not all good. Some of them are fakes. I once went to a *sangoma* in Benoni when my children were always passing away, passing away, when they were just born. My first two children were born in Marakabei and died after one day, one and a half days. The third time I am pregnant, when I arrive in Benoni where Alexis is, we go to a man, we call him 'Samonna,' a *sangoma* of men. When we arrive there, the *sangoma* takes his bones, he gives them to me and says I must throw them. I throw them. He says, 'Oh, this lady is sick because you didn't pay *lobola* for her. It's because her heart says you didn't pay *lobola* for her. So that's why these children are dying like this. Because she have no trust that you are ever going to pay *lobola* for her.'

I was very angry but I didn't let this man see my anger. Alexis had paid my *lobola* nicely, it was no question of that. But we did not say anything to this *sangoma*. And he gave us medicine, says 'You must drink this.' He put the medicine in the bottle and gave us another medicine for when we enter home. He says we must take a little coal from the fire in the house, and put this medicine on there so it can make a smoke, because the house we are staying in is not good. We do that. We take the fire and put the medicine.

That night we didn't sleep. There was something on the roof going up and down, and we never heard such things before. The medicine, I didn't even taste it. I told Alexis I don't want even to taste that medicine because that *sangoma* is a liar.

I say, 'How can he say you didn't pay *lobola*, because you did. And I know we are both worried about these children.' So I don't like this *sangoma*. I pour his medicine outside on the ground, and that medicine which he says I must put on the fire, I throw it in the toilet, never use it again. You have to be careful with *sangomas*. You have to use your own mind, and your feelings, to see if what they tell you makes sense.

In 1986 I went to a *sangoma* again.

One day I was going to work at the guest house. A lady passed me, said, '*Hei!* '*M'e* Mpho, you are always going late to work.'

I didn't pay attention. She always talks. But she puts her medicine on the path when I didn't see, and when I step over it I feel something bite me on the heel. But I didn't worry about it, I just went on to work.

One day I had a stomach-pain, it felt like something going up and down inside me. I stayed in bed, and I was sleeping the whole day. A girl from a nearby house came and asked me, '*'M'e* Mpho, why are you still sleeping?'

I say, 'My stomach is very sick. Something is going up and down.'

She says, 'I'm going to tell my mother.'

Her mother comes back with her and says, 'Let's go to see the *Bapostola* in the Police Station. It was an Apostolic healer who was also a policeman. When we arrive there the man says, 'It's only two days left till you are supposed to be dead. You passed where they put some medicine on the path and a wizard-snake bit you on the heel. It was sent by a lady who says she wants you to die because you are working, and your children are not working; but when your children come to you, drinking *joala* and being worthless, you give them food and a place to sleep, as if you are not tired of them. This lady says you make her look bad to her children. So she is going to kill you, because she wants your children to die.'

So this *Bapostola* doctor helps me and gives me water, only pure water. He prays over it and gives it to me. I drink it, and he tells me to take a bath in it. He calls a *Bapostola* lady to come and wash me in that water. After that, he gives me more water in a bottle and says, 'When you arrive at home, take the water in your hands and sprinkle the doorway and then the whole house. And you are going to sleep well. Tomorrow you must come again.'

When I left in the morning to go and see him, I couldn't walk well, only very slowly, leaning on my friend's arm. But when I arrive home I can walk. I even go to the garden and cook *moroho* for my children.

While I am cooking, there comes that lady who put her medicine out for me, and she says, ''*M'e* Mpho, where were you the whole day?'

I tell her I had stomach ache.

'Stomach ache? Even me, I had one too.'

I say, 'I think you are not so sick as I am. I went to a doctor, because I know this stomach ache is not God's sickness. I went to the doctor who told me what is going on, and I am going to tell my children where this sickness comes from. If I die from it, my children will know why.'

She was very quiet. Then her cat came. She is always walking with a cat. I said, 'I don't want this cat in my house.'

She says, 'Oh, cat, come.' I did not look her in the face. I was just cooking, not looking at her. She could see that something was wrong. So when I told her I wanted my children to know where this sickness came from, she said, 'Oh, I'm going now. *Sala hantle*. Good bye.'

I say, 'OK.'

The next day I go back to the doctor. I do the same things again. He gives me warm water, only pure water with nothing in it. He just prays over it. After that I take it, and I vomit. Then we put fresh water in the bath. The *Bapostola* woman washes me and prays, asks God to help *'M'e* Mpho with this sickness. I never met this lady before, but she prays hard for me.

I took seven days going to the police station for this treatment, and the last day they lit seven candles around the bath. I take a bath. The lady washes me. And I was almost healed. A few days after that, I am well, totally.

You are supposed to go to a *sangoma* when you are going on a trip or to a new town far away; you must go and check whether you are going to go have a good journey or something like that. But I never do it. I only go when I am sick or when I have problems in my house, maybe my children are sick. Then I go, and I see what happens.

In 1993 I am having many problems. I am building a nice new cement-block house with money which Limakatso has collected from many people in America who want to help me, and I see that many of my neighbours are jealous. I have pains in my body like a wizard-snake going up and down. My children are sick. Many things are going wrong. So first I go to a woman *sangoma* who lives near Mokhokhong, the home of my father's family. I make many trips to see this lady, and she gives me medicines, but these medicines don't help me.

Then I find a *sangoma* who is a young man who uses charms and herbs. He went to school in Durban to learn all of this, and he has two small beaded dolls called *balimo*; he calls them Grandfather and Grandmother, and these dolls talk to him. He says these dolls speak to us from our ancestors. The dolls tell him that I am surrounded by people who want me to die because they are so jealous. They say I have been poor all my life. Why should I have such a nice house now? They say they are going to kill me.

So the *sangoma* knows many things to do, to protect me, and my new house, and my children. He makes charms and buries them in the ground all around the foundation of my new house. He goes to the mountains for medicines for me to drink, and medicines for me to burn and sniff the smoke. He brings medicines for my children, and I think his medicines are very strong. We shall see.

CHAPTER 23

Limakatso and
the Beginning of this Book

A lady from America came to my guest house in August 1992, with four suitcases full of clothes. When I went to greet her and tell her my name, she said, 'Oh, you are going to help me!'

I say, 'Yes, *'M'e*, I will help you,' and I was still smiling like a fool, not knowing what she was going to do.

She takes the whole four suitcases and empties them on the bed and says, 'These clothes got very wrinkled in the bags. Please, can you iron them?'

I say, *'E 'M'e*, I'll iron them,' and I try not to look very surprised. She went away, and I ironed. All day I ironed. I did not even take time for tea or lunch. I stand on the left leg for a while; then I stand on the right leg. I think I have never seen so many clothes to iron for one person. At the end of the day I was half an hour past time to go home, and I was still not finished. I still have two dresses left. So I went home, very tired, wondering how long is this lady going to stay in the guest house.

The next day she comes home in the morning and finds me ironing those two dresses. She says, 'Oh, thank you very much, *'M'e*,' and she gave me some money. When she gave me the money I felt different. I was very glad to see that this person . . . she can stay with me here.

The next day she was working at home, and I could see that she was very cold. I thought, 'Oh shame. This lady doesn't know how to find wood for the fireplace. I must help her.' So I go and find wood and make a fire for her, and she thanks me very much.

The next day I do the same, because I know that it's cold and she doesn't know anything. She was sitting in the chair, curled up in a blanket, shivering, and trying to read. I saw she was sad, too, even when she didn't speak about it. She could not think well because she was so cold, and I saw that she would think many things. Maybe she misses her people in America. Maybe she is unhappy because of this cold in Lesotho.

One day she went to town for shopping, and she asked what she can bring me. I say, 'Cabbage.'

She says, 'What?'

I say, 'Cabbage.'

She looks very surprised. I don't know why. But she brings back two big cabbages, and I take them home. I told my children when I got home, 'The new *'M'e* in the guest house gave me these cabbages.'

So we give this lady the name Limakatso, which means someone who brings surprises, wonders, even miracles. And we didn't know, when we gave her this name, how many miracles she would bring. She was going to make more changes in my life than any *lekhooa* I ever knew.

It was her first time to come to Lesotho, even her first time to come anywhere in Africa, so she asked me many questions, and she asked me to teach her a little bit of Sesotho. I told her how to say the greetings, how to say *Lumela, Khotso*, and all of that. She took just one day and she learned them. But after that she was slow to learn Sesotho. She says it's hard to learn a new language when you are a grandmother, and even me, it is harder for me to learn new words now than when I was a girl, so we are patient with Limakatso.

One day I was having no paraffin, no *phofo*. I thought, 'What can I do? Can I go borrow the money from Limakatso?' But I was afraid. What if she would be angry, or tell me no? She was reading, and I went into the house and made a fire for her, all the time practising in my mind the words to say to her. I can't say anything. I go out and I come back. We talk about many things. She asks me where I live, how many children do I have. I am afraid of her. Maybe she asks these questions because she can see what is in my mind. I go into her bathroom and stand there. I have nothing to do in that bathroom. It's clean. I come out again, and my mouth will not speak these things my mind is telling me to say. I just say, 'I must go home now, *'M'e*.'

I go home and pray my God not to let me be so shy the next day.

So the next day Limakatso seems happy to see me. She is working at home again, and we talk, talk. When it is time for me to go home I say, 'Oh, *'M'e*, forgive me. Can you borrow me fifty rands? I will return the money when I find my pay from the University.'

She says, 'Oh, why? What's the matter?'

I tell her the University pays me very late every month, and my children have nothing to eat.

She doesn't refuse. She just goes to get the money from her bag and gives it to me. She says, 'How many children do you have living at home with you?'

I say, 'Nine.'

'And these are your grandchildren?'

I say 'Yes.'

'Is there anyone else living with you?'

I say 'My daughter-in-law, who was married to my son who died in 1987. 'M'athuso has no work; she stays at home.'

'How much money does the University pay you?'

I say three hundred thirty rands a month. Limakatso looks very much surprised.

'How can you feed all these people on that little money?'

I say sometimes we have no food.

'No food at all? Nothing?'

I say 'Yes, even now. For three days we have no food. The children are crying with hunger.' So she says I must take that fifty rands and keep it, not pay it back when my cheque comes from the University. So we started to be friends.

I say, 'Your name is good for you, Limakatso. I don't know where you come from. Maybe God sends you to me. Or maybe it's my mother, who asks God to send you to me.'

One Saturday I was with my neighbours, going to a funeral. I saw Limakatso in the village, trying to take people's photographs. One of my neighbours shook her head and said 'No!' to Limakatso. I saw that these people were going to make her sad. We were all walking in a queue, and I stepped out of the queue and greeted my friend. I could see she was very surprised to see me, and very glad. She asked me where were all these ladies going, and I told her it was a funeral. She didn't know. So she said she would put her camera away until all the people for the funeral were gone. She was going up the mountain, walking alone, making photos, and I showed her my house and said she could come meet my children, and she could take their photos; I would be happy for that. So that is how she began to come visit me at my house.

In September she moved out of the guest house, to her own flat on the campus, and I sent her my niece, Nthabiseng, to work as her helper, and Nthabiseng's mother to work in her garden, and we began to eat lunch together every day, all of us. Limakatso always likes me to come and eat with them, no matter I am not working with her. I stop at her house when I am going home from work every day, and we talk many things.

That day of the funeral, Limakatso went all the way up the mountain, to a house of an old lady who was living there alone in a little mud house with a thatched roof. Limakatso took a picture of this house, and another time she asked me if I could walk with her to give the old lady the picture and to meet her.

Limakatso says, 'I want to meet the old lady who lives alone in this little mud house. I have a feeling about her. Can you come and translate, if I give you a little money for it?'

I say Yes, because I need the money. I don't know this old lady, because her house is very far up the mountain. Limakatso buys a cabbage and some sugar, to give to the old lady when we arrive, and she carries these things in a plastic bag all the way up. When we find the house, after walking maybe an hour uphill, we meet the old lady, who is very poor. She has no shoes; her blanket is torn and thin; she has a cough, and her skin hangs on her bones like rags.

She is very surprised to see this cabbage and this bag of sugar. She laughs and claps her hands; she says God has sent this lady to her, because she was starving, just about to die from hunger. She speaks no English at all, not even one word, and Limakatso speaks no Sesotho except to say the greetings, but I translate for her and for Limakatso. Then we show her the photo of her house, and she laughs again. She cannot see anything special about her house; she looks at Limakatso like she is a miracle.

Then Limakatso begins to ask questions. The old lady says she is *'M'e* 'M'alebohang, and she built that house herself, alone, twelve years ago when she was only sixty and came home to Lesotho from the Republic, where she was making and selling *joala*. 'M'alebohang says to Limakatso, 'I need work. Do you have any work for me?'

Limakatso says, 'What can you do?'

The old lady laughs.

'Can you sew? Can you make pots? Can you make grass mats?'

No. The old lady says she can do none of these things. She says she is old. I was not telling Limakatso the old lady doesn't really want work. She just wants money, but she is too proud to beg for it.

So Limakatso says, 'I don't know how I can help you, *'M'e*,' and she looks very worried. We all stand quiet together. I look out to the mountains. Then suddenly an idea comes to Limakatso, and she smiles very big. 'Oh, *'M'e*! I know. You can tell me stories, and I can write them down, and I can pay you for them.'

'M'e 'M'alebohang says, 'I don't know any stories.'

'Stories of your life,' Limakatso says, like this is a thing which can happen every day. 'Tell me what happened to you in your life, and in your mother's life. And I will write this down, and I can give you money for this.'

I am just translating. I can see *'M'e* 'M'alebohang thinks Limakatso is a crazy someone, but at the same time she is good, because she brings cabbage and sugar, and she finds a way to give 'M'alebohang work when there is nothing 'M'alebohang can do. So we say we will come back the next week, and Limakatso will bring a book to write the stories in.

So we go back the next week. When we arrive, 'M'alebohang's sister, who is also very poor and starving, so bad she has a disease which makes her skin look burnt, comes to tell stories too, and we all work together for maybe two hours. Limakatso writes down everything, but I think, 'Shame! these old women are living alone for a long time, and they don't know how to talk much or tell stories.'

Limakatso asks many questions, but the old women just say the same thing over and over: 'We were very poor. We had nothing to eat, nothing to wear. All our life it was this way, and it is this way now.'

So Limakatso gives ten rands to 'M'alebohang, and ten rands to her sister, and later she gives me twenty rands for translating, and I am happy for this little bit of money. But when we are walking back down the mountain, I begin to tell Limakatso my mother's story, the story of how we moved to Benoni because of a dream that came to my father three times.

Limakatso says, ''M'e, this is exactly what I want. You are a wonderful storyteller.'

I don't know what she wants stories for; I think she is just looking for a way to give us money so we don't feel ashamed. I have told my mother's story many times to my children and my grandchildren, always in Sesotho. Never in English. But I find I can tell the story in English, too. So that's how we begin to make this book, and from there, we never went again to 'M'alebohang for stories. Limakatso still goes to see her and gives her money sometimes, but I have no more time to go up and down to get 'M'alebohang's one little sad story. Instead I begin to come to Limakatso's house every Sunday to tell my stories, and she writes them all down in exercise books, and she gives me seventy rands every week.

For a long time this was just a game to me. Then one day Limakatso typed some of the stories on her computer and showed me the pages. The first time I read my words typed on paper, I was so surprised, it was like a miracle to me.

'Did I really say this?' I asked her.

'Aren't these your words?' she asked me back.

I say, 'Yes.'

'And isn't this your story?'

I say, 'Yes.'

'Did I know that story before you told it to me?'

I say, 'No.'

'Then whose words can they be, but your words?'

I laughed when I saw that it was real, that my words could look like words in a book, and maybe my stories could be a book that other people could read. At about the same time, Limakatso got me a little book of stories told by a Zulu lady, so I could see how it is done. I knew my book was already bigger than that one, and my stories were better to listen to.

Another time Limakatso took me to Maseru, to meet the writers there who were coming to a class Limakatso was teaching. And they read one of my stories out loud, and they read some of their stories, and I find that I'm a better writer than some of them. They talk English better; they speak many words I don't understand, because they have all been to University and I only speak simple English, but I can see that my stories are better to listen to. I begin to believe that with God's help, I can write a book. Every time Limakatso types one of my stories, I want to read every word of it. But I was having trouble with my eyes, and I would get a headache when I try to read. I look very hard at the paper, but everything looks gray sometimes.

In December Limakatso wanted to go on holiday to Durban, and she asked me to go. I say I have worked at the guest house from 1980 until today, and I have never had a holiday, and she says I must come and see the ocean, so we get permission from the University for me to be off work for a week, and we go together.

It was my first time to see the ocean. We would go to the ocean and sit there, watch the water until we were tired, and then go back to the hotel and look at television. I saw television a few times in Ha Lepota's store, but I did not watch it for a long time, just while I was doing my shopping. I find I love to look at the television. And the ocean is a big surprise to me, too. I thought the ocean was a river, a big river. But when I saw it, I saw that I don't know where it starts and ends. It's so big I'm afraid to walk in it. I did walk by it and let the water wash over my feet, because Limakatso said I must do this, but I felt it pull me on the sand, and I was afraid.

While we were in Durban, Limakatso said we must go see an eye doctor. Maybe I need new spectacles. The ones I had were from 1986. So we went to a doctor some lady recommended to us, in Westville, which is a place where many white people live, outside of Durban. This doctor's office is in a big hospital, very nice, with carpet on the floors, and pictures on the walls, and real flowers on the table, and magazines that are not too old. The white doctor looks at my eyes and talks nicely to us, explaining everything. He says I am blind in one eye and almost blind in the other one. He says it's too bad, they used to have student doctors who go to Lesotho to make the operation on people like me, but they don't go there anymore. He says I am going to be blind, totally, in six months or a year.

I can hear in Limakatso's voice, she is beginning to be angry with this doctor. I don't say anything, I am just watching them, and I can feel my heart beating very hard. I think of my mother. She used to pray every night, 'Please God, don't let me be blind,' and she never was blind. But now I am going to be blind.

Limakatso says, 'Can you make this operation?'

The doctor says 'Yes, but it will cost very much money.'

She asks him how much.

I don't even want to say how much he told her. We were staying in the hotel, eating money and drinking money, every-thing is money, and he says it will take more money than I ever saw, to make this operation on my eyes.

She looks at me and says, softly, *"M'e* Mpho, are you willing for this doctor to make the operation on your eyes?'

I can't find my voice to speak. I just nod my head, Yes. And so we fix the time. The very next day I am going to have this operation.

When I arrived at the hospital, it was my first time to have an operation since I was born. All the people in this hospital are white people, except the cleaning women. The nurses are white, the patients are white, the doctors are white. I feel very shy. The nurses ask me when I have had an operation, and I say 'No. Never.' I was frightened. They say my blood pressure was very high: two hundred over something. They give me some orange pills to make it go down. Limakatso goes with me, and she stands beside the bed and holds my hand when they ask me questions and take my blood pressure. She helps me do what they tell me. There is so much roaring in my ears sometimes I can't hear what the nurses say.

They say I must take off all my clothes, even my panties, and put on paper ones. Paper dress, paper hat, even paper panties. This feels very strange, and I don't know why I am doing these things, but I do them. Limakatso takes my watch and my bracelets and says she will keep them for me. I wonder if I am going to be alive after this, to put them back on. Maybe they are going to kill me. They put me on a bed with wheels and they take me away from Limakatso and leave me in a hallway where I have to look up at the ceiling, waiting for another person to be finished with the operation. I am waiting there for two hours, very much afraid.

The nurses were very nice to me in this time. Sometimes they talk Zulu with me, and I answer them in Zulu. Then the doctor hears them. He says, 'This lady comes from Lesotho. She doesn't speak Zulu. You must talk English with her.'

But he goes away, and the nurse says, 'Do you know Zulu?'

I say, '*Yebo*, I know it.'

'The doctor says you only know English.'

I say, 'That doctor doesn't know anything about me,' and we laugh.

Finally it is my time for the operation. The doctor puts an injection in my eye. I see the needle coming, but it doesn't hurt me. The doctor talks to me softly, very nice, and tells me not to be afraid. I don't say anything. He takes my eye and sellotapes it open, and he takes my eyeball out. He grunts and strains like he is skinning a sheep, and I see he is working very hard, but I don't feel anything. Even when he takes the scissors and cuts, I don't feel anything, but I see his hand moving on my eye. When he is finished he says to the nurses, 'This was a very nice operation. No problems at all. This is a nice lady, and her operation goes very quickly.'

So they roll my bed out, and they push it back to the room where Limakatso is waiting. I find my clothes again, and I put my watch and my bracelets back on. It seems like a very long time ago that I took them off. After the operation I was not supposed to bend over or walk without a person to help me. The nurses were talking, they say, 'Your *molongu* (that is the Zulu word for *lekhooa*) was asking about you. Are you working for this lady?'

I say, 'No. It's my friend only.'

They say, 'She loves you very much.'

I say, 'I know.'

They check my blood pressure, and it is a little bit better.

Other ladies came, the cleaning ladies, and it was good to see black faces. They speak to me in Zulu and tell me I am the first black person they have seen in this hospital who was not cleaning the floor. It was a white hospital, and we didn't know it. Limakatso just laughs, and she holds my hand.

The cleaning ladies ask me if I am working for her, and I say, 'No. She is my friend.' We think it is good for them to see us loving each other, and we go home. It all happened in just one day, and that night Limakatso brought me two roses and put them in a water glass on the table by the window where we look at the ocean. It was my first time anybody gave me roses.

The next day we have to come again to see the doctor. He takes off the cotton wool which was in front of my eye, and everything is very bright and clear in that eye, like a miracle. He asks me, 'Does it hurt?'

I say 'No.' I don't feel anything wrong. It was a good operation. He says I have to wear the cotton wool over my eye for a few more days, but I am not going to be blind at all. I begin to feel how tired I am, from so many things which have happened to me for the first time, in just a few days. And from there, I thought about my mother again, and I thought it was my mother who sent Limakatso to me so I would not be blind. Now I am waiting for a time when my eyes are good enough that I can sit down and read my own book.

CHAPTER 24

The Time for New Dreams

When I was a little girl, lying in the rondavel waiting for my mother to come home with a handful of mealies, I had the dreams of a child. I dreamed: when I grow up, if God can help me, I'm going to be rich like other people. I see the rich children. They have shoes and clothes, and they have food in their houses that they don't even eat before they sleep. When they wake up in the morning there is food for the whole day, no worries. I want to be like that. When I grow up I'll be rich, and I will buy food to sit on the shelf, and dresses for my mother, and a beautiful rosary for her to pray.

When I was a schoolgirl in Benoni, walking to school with my books in my arms, I was dreaming sweetly: when I'm married I will be married to a rich man with a car, and I will help my mother. I will stay with my mother, so that she can eat nice food like my rich husband and me. I will buy her dresses, and take her for rides in our car.

When I was in Marakabei with my fields and my children and my sheep, at the end of the day, I would sit in front of the rondavel and watch the sun going down. I would dream, then, to have good crops and many sheep and cows, so I can help my mother. I would sit and think of my mother, because she was far from me, and very poor. And I would worry. I was thinking sometimes, 'Oh, my mother, maybe she is hungry. Maybe she is sick and there is no one to take her to a doctor. Maybe she has died, and there is no way for anybody to bring me the message.'

Sometimes I would think so hard that I would even cry, and I wondered when I was going to my mother's house to see her again.

After Alexis died, when I was working at Mrs Masongo's

160

house, at the end of the day when I went to my little room in the back of her house, I would dream. At that time I wanted to have a house and stay with my children, because I was tired of staying in other people's houses. I always thought about that. When I entered in the lavatory, I used to cry and say, 'Oh, God, if you can give me just a little house the size of this lavatory, it can be better for me.'

I remember one Saturday when I went home to see my mother and the children, I told my mother, 'Oh, I'm tired of having no house. I know that I've got my houses in Marakabei, so it's better to me to take my children and go away.'

And my mother says, '*Oa hlanya*! You are mad. How can you leave your work and go to the mountains with no man to help you, just for a house? God will help you. You will have a house.'

I say 'No. It takes too much time. When did I start to pray God to help me to find a house?'

She says, 'You know that you worked for a only a few months and then Alexis died and you had to go away for your mourning time; so now you must stay and work hard, and in time you will find a house.'

I was very cross that day. My mother was just telling me to pray, and I didn't want even to answer her. My mother says, 'I think you don't trust God. You trust yourself, and you can't see how you will find a house by yourself.'

And it was true. I was angry with God. I was angry because of not having a house. It seemed like there was no God. In my heart, for that little time right after Alexis died, I thought God was not there. I didn't say this to my mother, but she knew.

The next day when she woke up, my mother took her rosary and went to the Mass, at six o'clock. She did this for nine days, going to the church every morning at six. I didn't know what she was praying, but by the end of that nine days, the doubt went away from my mind and I knew again that God was there, and that God would help me, in time.

And that did happen. I got *lobola* for Manraile, and I took the money and bought rafters, and my children collected the stones from the mountains, and in time I made a house, the same house I am living in now. When that house was finished, my mother asked me again, 'Do you still think God is not there? Do you see how God helps you?'

I say I'm sorry. I did not know she was thinking all that time that I was doubting God. I say, 'It's because at that time I was angry. But long ago I watched you making Novena, and I knew again that God is there and he would help me one day.'

She says, 'Yes. When you are in trouble you must always say, "God help me." Don't trust yourself.'

I say 'Oh, *ke hantle*. I understand from today.'

I know God can't come at the same time when you are asking, and he can't just come and reach out his hand into your life and give to you. The thing you want will come, if it's God's will, and if you do something to help it come. And when it comes, maybe you can't see that it comes from God. Maybe you think it's because you are clever. But it's God, working with you, and you, working with God.

I'm still dreaming, but now I laugh and dream at the same time. My husband has gone to see God, and my mother, and my babies, and those three grown sons. I know I will die too, when it is time. So there is nothing to be afraid of. I laugh at myself, because I'm still thinking I want to be rich, have plenty of food for all my grandchildren, shoes and school fees, money for doctors if we are sick. I find myself saying if I can have a house with a fence, I will lock the gate when I sleep. I dream that this book will go far, and tell people about the Basotho, how it is with us, how poor we are and how we go on with life anyway. I dream many things, but the dreams are gentle ones. They don't shout at the sky. If they can come true, fine; if they cannot come true, another thing will happen, as God wants.

I know I cannot sit still and wait for God to help me. I must be helping myself as much as I can. I work with my hands. I know that these grandchildren must have education; we cannot always be cleaning houses and working for *phofo*. I look at my village, and I see how the people are living, and I know something is wrong: so much hunger, so many people needing work, so many people drinking *joala* when they have a little bit of money, and so much jealousy everywhere, because there is never enough of anything.

There is work we must do in Lesotho to help ourselves. South Africa is changing. The Boer laws are passing away, and now Nelson Mandela is President of South Africa. I never thought I would see this in my life, and I am happy to live at this time and to see this. But these changes are not all good for the Basotho. The Basotho miners are coming home, retrenched, and they find no work here. School fees are going up, and more children are staying at home. When our children do go to school, they are not learning to speak *Sekhooa*, the white people's language. There are no jobs for people who cannot speak *Sekhooa*. You cannot even get a job cleaning houses or working in people's gardens unless you speak English.

The students who used to come to our university from South Africa can go to their own universities now, and many of our lecturers are going away. They can make more money in South Africa. There is less work for the women in my village because we depend on the university. I am cleaning the guest house, and I see these things, because all the women in the village come to me. They say, *''M'e* Mpho, you must help us to find work with the new people that come.' But there are many women wanting work, and few new people coming; the new people that come have many children and small money. They leave after two years. We had elections in 1993, and the Congress Party won. I have hope that our new government knows what to do to help all of this.

We can all have new dreams. I cannot see the end of them, or how they will be, but I know that our new dreams can go beyond shoes and houses and food to sit on the shelf. The new dreams cannot be only for one family, or one clan. Maybe if there is one day enough for the hunger to stop, we can stop being so jealous of one another. If the jealousy is no more, we can begin to have dreams for each other. We can build something new. It can be. If we are building something new, we can ask God to help us, and we will be busy while we are asking. I think God likes to help people who are already busy, working for their dreams.

Afterword

By K. Limakatso Kendall

Mpho 'M'atsepo Nthunya was supporting eleven people on her salary as a 'casual laborer' at the National University of Lesotho when I met her. I was in Lesotho as a Senior Fulbright Scholar, teaching creative writing and English literature. She had been scrubbing and polishing floors, washing sheets and blankets, and doing personal laundry for a stream of expatriates at the university guest house since 1980. More importantly, as the ruling elder of a large African family, she had long been the keeper and re-teller of the family's stories and history.

I came to her hungry for stories of African life because of the specific tracery of unconnected adventures which are my own life's story. I was born in North Carolina and spent the first five years of my life shuttling between the white community where I lived with my grandparents, and the black community where my grandfather worked as a shop assistant in a hardware store. Racism moulded my earliest seeing and hearing, but the stories I heard in the hardware store braided with the stories my great-grandmother told me and filled me with wonder and admiration. I started writing when a long bout of rheumatic fever confined me to bed from the time I was six till I was eight. My first stories were attempts to recapture the splendour, the drama, and the beauty of the tales I had heard from black and white story-tellers.

Later on I concentrated on creative writing for the ten years it took me to complete my BA, and I spent the years between 1973 and 1990 doing research and creative projects involving orality, storytelling, and performance. My MA thesis in 1975 was a placename survey compiled from oral histories, and I toured the USA. in 1980 with a one-woman show called *Characters*, which was my performance of stories told to me by a variety of women of different colours, ages, and backgrounds. My Ph.D. dissertation concerned women playwrights of the Queen Anne period in England, and again I created a performance piece, *This Panting Breast*, to illustrate the work in a live medium. When I taught at Smith College, in the USA, and began research in the archives there, I found a collection of letters by a nineteenth-century woman which seemed to 'speak' from the page; in 1990 I created a one-woman play called *Dear Little Weed* in which I performed those letters. My whole life has focused on oral and written stories and storytelling, so when 'M'e Mpho first told me the story of the dream that came three times, I heard it with trained ears, and I recognised it as a product of genius.

'M'e Mpho speaks eight languages, remembers in graphic detail all the many lives she has led, and weaves tales with the skill of a traditional Mosotho storyteller. With her ability, had she been born to another race, another class, another gender, or in another place, she might have been a world-reknowned author, a business executive, a university president, a saint. With her love of books, she would certainly have earned a college degree, or two or three.

Perhaps I will sometime tell the story of our relationship and of the effect this book has had on both of us. Me: a middle-aged white American woman, a university teacher with a Ph.D. and an erratic life which has included many loves, many jobs, many travels, two sons, and two adopted daughters. She: a dignified and gracious Mosotho widow in her mid-sixties with a primary-school education. Once a prosperous farmer with two hundred sheep and many fields, she turned to domestic service in 1968, when her husband died and she had to support the family. We met as two grandmothers born fifteen years apart in different worlds on opposite sides of the planet. We are unlikely though devoted friends.

'M'e Mpho never really believed that her stories could be made into a book. She laughed at me throughout the years while we worked on it, driven primarily by my obsession to make it happen, and secondarily by her amused curiosity to discover what such a thing might mean. She humoured me, patiently recounting her stories, pausing for me to catch up. As she explains in the text, she dictated the book to me. I wrote it in the improvised shorthand I developed when I worked as a secretary, in several exercise books (which I have saved), and then I transcribed it onto computer disks. I would print out a chapter, give it to her to read, and then discuss it with her. We would add and delete, rearrange paragraphs or sentences, prune and polish, pausing again and again for her to read or perform each new version aloud. Her process is more auditory than literary, and she liked hearing her own words and couldn't decide if a paragraph 'worked' until she heard herself speak it. I didn't save the original hard copies, so there is no record of the editing process which took place in the computer. We settled on a 'final' version of the stories in June 1993. I sent it off to one publisher and then another, and she went on cleaning the guest house and forgot about it.

As I was working with 'M'e Mpho on weekends throughout 1992 and 1993, I was discussing in my classrooms at the National University of Lesotho the politics of language. I studied with Ngugi wa Thiong'o before coming to Lesotho, and I made his book, *Decolonising the Mind*, the basis for one of my courses. In that book Ngugi explains why he writes his novels in Kikuyu and then translates them into English. He defines an African novel as a novel written by an African person in an African language. He calls his earlier novels written in English 'Afro-European' novels. He champions African orature because 'it has its roots in the lives of the peasantry. It is primarily their compositions, their songs, their art, which forms the basis of the national and resistance culture' (*Decolonising the Mind*, p.95).

I believe that 'M'e Mpho, coming from a tradition of African orature and having told many of these stories before, in Sesotho, was actually thinking and hearing her tales in Sesotho and spontaneously translating them into English. It was not, from her standpoint, an ideal or comfortable arrangement. 'I wish I could tell you this in Sesotho,' she said again and again, in the face of my ignorance of her language and my limping and ineffectual efforts to learn it. Yet her struggle to translate the stories verbally into English condensed them, tightened them, and may have made them more powerful in some ways than the Sesotho originals. We once tried a different system: '*M'e* Mpho told a story in Sesotho and our very good friend, Julia Chere-Masopha, who is fully bilingual in English and Sesotho, translated it into English. Julia's translation of '*M'e* Mpho's story was much less powerful in English than '*M'e* Mpho's own translation, so we decided to stick with '*M'e* Mpho's English.

'*M'e* Mpho speaks a new language in these stories. It's not the 'Queen's English'; it's not an African language; and it isn't a unique language with its own rules, like pidgin, or certain forms of West Indian English. It is a form of English spoken only in Lesotho, with idioms that arise from literal translation of Sesotho expressions, with a vocabulary peppered with Sesotho words, with a rhythm and with inflections all its own. I scrupulously avoided 'correcting' '*M'e* Mpho's English. The tenses are irregular, though I notice there is a definite pattern: when she is remembering with some distance, she uses the past tense; when the memories become vivid and immediate, she shifts to the present.

I pondered our ethical dilemma. *In Male Daughters, Female Husbands*, an Igbo scholar, Ifi Amadiume, regrets that 'most of the data on African women which is available to Black women in the West has been collected by White women' (p. 7). She observes, '. . . collecting and publishing what Third World women are saying . . . is another form of exploitation' (p. 10). I know that has sometimes been the case, although I determined it would not be so with us. My intention was to put my privilege at '*M'e* Mpho's disposal without usurping her authorship, her rights, or what will (I hope) eventually be her profits. The University of Natal Press has promised '*M'e* Mpho fifty percent of the proceeds from the sales of this book after production costs. '*M'e* Mpho's vision is failing, she has no patience for reading proofs, and she is not interested in editorial decisions such as when to use italics or where to insert paragraph breaks. Therefore she and I have agreed to give me billing as her 'editor', though it is necessary to qualify what exactly, in our case, that means.

My contribution was, first, to hear the stories and to believe in their artistic and cultural importance; then to evoke a full rendering of them from her by listening and questioning with respect and enjoyment; to put her words on the paper so others could hear them speak; to discuss each story with her and to assist her in crafting each story into a shape which she thinks works on paper; to arrange the stories in some kind of order; and finally to locate a publisher, to negotiate a contract, and to shepherd the work into book form. As she explains in her own text, she had no idea how to get her stories written down, let alone how to find a publisher. As a woman with almost no experience of books in her own life, she could not imagine such a thing as authorship of a book. She still laughs at the idea.

My contribution was not trivial. I held the vision of 'M'e Mpho's stories as a book in my heart and head for nearly four years, from the beginning of our work together in September 1992, to the release of the volume in 1996. I spent far more hours typing, re-typing, arranging, marketing, editing, and proof-reading the material than 'M'e Mpho spent telling me the stories. I was editor, agent, and advocate; I took care of the business of getting the book out. However the artistic activity was all hers. She lived the stories; she created and told them; and she was the person who decided, finally, exactly what would be told and what would not, and how each story would be told.

'M'e Mpho has a knack for generating suspense at the beginnings of her stories and for tying them together at the end with a line or two that harks back to the beginning. The stories came out in no particular order, often in response to my questions, to current family events, to our travels together in the mountains where she once lived, or to memories coming to light by chance. I have chosen the order for the presentation of the stories so that they loosely shape themselves into a kind of autobiography. She agreed to that shape, shrugging her shoulders. She feels no need for a linear or chronological narrative, and to her mind there is no reason why any one story should precede or follow another. The stories overlap, spiral around each other, and come back again and again to the spare and powerful images of 'M'e Mpho's life and to her memories of her mother, whom she credits with teaching her how to live and how, literally, to sing the hunger away.

There is a proverb in Sesotho, '*Motho ke motho ka batho*', which means a person is a person because s/he is of the people. We are one. Identities are intertwined. The Basotho have long been a communal people, and although that communality is breaking down under global pressures, urbanisation, and other facets of life in the late twentieth century, many Basotho still live in community, define their lives by their roles in community, and even create in community. Music echoes with call and response. Dance is a participatory and not a spectator activity. Speeches build on murmurs of assent, understanding, agreement. A story-teller evokes a listener, and a listener helps to shape the story. The children women carry on their backs bring stories into being as fully as the women do when they select words for the telling. They create together, listener and speaker. Nthunya presumes a kind of hearer who can and will contribute what one might call the 'politics' or the messages imbedded in the tales. She never tells the reader/listener what to feel, or what she felt. She evokes feelings, responses, questions in the reader. She leaves the process of synthesis to a reader who is presumed to be sympathetic.

On the way to publication I encountered some readers who doubted the authenticity of the stories. Most asked how much I had tampered with the manuscript or intervened in 'M'e Mpho's telling of the stories. It is certainly true that whenever 'M'e Mpho paused in her telling, I asked questions. My own background as a writer and a teacher of creative writing, drama, and women's studies, must have dictated some of those questions. They are the questions I ask myself and my university students as we create drafts of our stories or as we rehearse our plays: What time of day was it? What was he wearing? What did you say then? What was she doing when you said that to her? How did you feel when that happened? What did your eyes see when you entered the room? What did it smell like? How long did you wait? These questions led to the elaboration of some stories and sometimes unleashed whole new stories, but all the stories are hers, authentically.

I worked as a medical and academic secretary for eleven years on my way to becoming an academic myself, and during those years I frequently wrote down, for the first time, letters, papers, dissertations, and books spoken into a dictaphone by men with more education than I then had. I contributed spelling, punctuation, and paragraphing. I sometimes reorganised sections or paragraphs. I added section titles and headings. None of those writers ever mentioned me as his editor, and none ever asked me to write an introduction to material he published with my help. Therefore I have chosen not to write an introduction to *'M'e* Mpho's book. I intervened less in her process than in the processes of the men whose secretary I was in the 1960s and 1970s.

Given the context of racism and classism in which we all live, it is reasonable that people at various points on the political spectrum might question whether these stories are authentic, though no one ever questioned whether articles by the male professors for whom I worked in a similar sphere were authentic. Misogynistic critics have often questioned the authenticity of even very famous women's writing and have suggested that if it was good, a man probably wrote it for her or helped her write it. Some white women, presuming to speak for black women, have used those black women as a front for their own white voices or have justified their exploitation of those black women by claiming they were only 'helping' the black woman express herself.

Carole Boyce-Davies, a Trinidadian scholar who is a specialist in autobiography and writing by women of colour and whom I met at a conference just after the University of Natal Press had agreed to publish the book, suggested that I 'problematise' myself as rather more than a typist. I see her point. My experience as a scribe and performer of orature and as a writer of short stories, as a university teacher of theatre and creative writing, as an American working-class woman moving into the middle class, all influenced the questions I asked *'M'e* Mpho, and the way she framed her answers or told her stories. My white privilege shaped my hearing and must have influenced her telling. It is likely that the stories would have emerged differently if an African woman had been recording them. Perhaps there are hidden aspects of the stories which would have surfaced; perhaps some of what is told would have been left out.

All of us who tell stories sometimes subtly (and sometimes blatantly) shape our stories to fit the audience, tell the parts we think our listeners want to hear, leave out what we fear would offend, explain what we think is not self-evident to the listeners. Therefore it is important that I identify myself as *'M'e* Mpho's auditor. Perhaps there is more about myself I could tell or should mention, to further 'problematise' myself in the text, but this is her book: and that is my final and most important point. This is her book.

Glossary

abuti:	brother, young man.
ausi:	sister, young woman.
balimo:	spirits of people who are dead.
Bapostola:	members of the Apostolic church.
bohale:	fierce, strong.
doek:	the Afrikaans word for a woman's head-scarf; also *tubu*.
hantle:	nice, nicely, well; *ke hantle*: fine.
ho lokile:	fine, OK.
huisie:	a square or rectangular traditional thatch-roofed house.
joala:	home-made beer.
khotso:	peace; also a greeting, *Khotso!*
lehlanya:	crazy person; pl., *bahlanya*: crazy people, they are crazy.
lekhooa:	white person; pl., *makhooa*: white people; *sekhooa*: white people's language.
lekoele:	liquid, especially home-made beer at a certain stage of the brewing.
lekoerekoere:	a black African who is not from southern Africa; pl., *makoerekoere*.
leloala:	a grinding stone.
lihobe:	a dish made of dried peas and maize meal.
lipina tsa mokopu:	songs of girls playing.
lisiu:	a large basket.
lobola:	bride-price; paid by the groom's family to the bride's family.

lumela:	the most common greeting; literally, it means, 'Do you agree?'; used to say 'Hello'.
'M'e:	literally, mother; a term of respect for any mature woman.
mafi:	sour milk.
Maxhosa:	Xhosa-speaking people.
mobu:	dirt.
moroho:	green, usually leafy, vegetables.
motoho:	non-alcoholic drink made from ground sorghum.
molamu:	a large stick which can be a walking-stick or a weapon.
motsoalle:	a very close friend.
naheng:	open fields for grazing.
nkhono:	grandmother.
ntate:	father; a term of respect for any mature man.
papa:	maize meal and water, cooked into a thick porridge.
patsi:	firewood.
phofo:	meal (usually maize meal); *phofo ea poone*, maize meal; *phofo ea koro*, wheat meal; *phofo ea mabele*, sorghum meal.
rakhali:	paternal aunt.
rondavel:	a round thatched-roof house.
samp:	a form of maize.
sangoma:	traditional healer.
selapa:	a shirt made of flannelette material which is worn by pregnant women in the last months of their pregnancies.
seshoeshoe:	a dark cloth with a white print design, made in England but so popular among Basotho women that it has come to be regarded as their 'traditional' dress.
thethana:	skirt of beads or string worn by young girls.
thokolosi:	evil spirit.

thotobolo:	ash-heap, or the dump where ashes from the fireplace are thrown.
tsotsi:	a gangster or crook.
tubu:	a headscarf or headwrap.
uena:	you.

Note on Gauteng

Gauteng is a Sesotho name meaning 'Place of Gold'. (Compare the Zulu name, Egoli.) It was used by Basotho to denote Johannesburg, the Witwatersrand or even South Africa. In 1994 Gauteng became the official name of the province that includes Johannesburg and the Witwatersrand, created from part of what was formerly the Transvaal.